VISIONARY LEADERSHIP

Learning to Lead from the Inside Out

BY

STEPHEN R. MASON

DORRANCE
PUBLISHING CO
EST. 1920
PITTSBURGH, PENNSYLVANIA 15238

The contents of this work, including, but not limited to, the accuracy of events, people, and places depicted; opinions expressed; permission to use previously published materials included; and any advice given or actions advocated are solely the responsibility of the author, who assumes all liability for said work and indemnifies the publisher against any claims stemming from publication of the work.

Dorrance Publishing Co
585 Alpha Drive
Pittsburgh, PA 15238
Visit our website at *www.dorrancebookstore.com*

ISBN: 978-1-6442-6018-0
eISBN: 978-1-6442-6045-6

I dedicate this book to my loving wife, Wanda, and daughter, Amanda, without whose support this book would not be possible.

ACKNOWLEDGMENTS

THIS BOOK WAS HALF A LIFETIME AND A CAREER IN THE MAKING, so acknowledgments fall into several categories. I must thank my family, starting with my parents, who gave me the opportunities to achieve the necessary tools for success. Next, my wife and daughter, for their patience throughout my career. The many people who challenged and mentored me to get better at what I did and nurtured the potential that they saw in me. The many leaders in every organization that I work in who were inspired to accept my vision and who are truly the reason those visions achieved success. Leadership is important, but success is not possible without the commitment of the hardworking people who day in and day out serve our patients and customers in a professional, high quality, and compassionate way. I must thank Kristen Sweeney for her commitment to the development, research, editing, and writing that gave me the opportunity to get my thoughts organized and the flow of the book out of my head and onto paper.

Finally, I want to acknowledge all of you, who have chosen a leadership path and are continuously looking for ways to expand and perfect the skills necessary to succeed in this very complicated world. Although your journey is different than mine, I hope this book is of some help in your quest.

FOREWORD

IN THIS BOOK, Steve Mason has captured the essence of visionary leadership in a variety of well-thought out, easily understood ways. To a great degree, he has demystified what many people deem to be mystifying abilities of visionary leaders.

This is far beyond a "how to" or a "Visionary Leadership for Dummies" book. Steve's insights relate to the source of visionary leadership: the subconscious mind. He dives into the many sources of creativity and in a logical, descriptive way, explains how the component particles of our mind and universe combine to develop visionary leaders.

Steve's career success as a visionary leader gives him the credibility necessary to authoritatively write about such an interesting and complex topic. His writing style is clear, concise and friendly which is exactly what one would expect from a visionary leader. Since this book is so full of valuable information, I highly recommend reading it multiple times. Having done so myself, I find additional valuable practical insights with each reading.

I believe Steve's perspectives are so important that I have made this book required reading for all our employees who are selected to participate in the leadership training curriculum within the Key Family of Companies. The feedback from our leadership candidates has been extraordinarily positive.

For all who want to look around the corner to the future and visualize what's next for their companies, Visionary Leadership is a must read. Here's to all who have the courage to embrace our imaginations and to lead into the future. Steve is a very effective Messenger–in–Chief.

Larry R. Dust
CEO
Key Family of Companies

TABLE OF CONTENTS

INTRODUCTION

"Every strike brings me closer to the next home run."

–Babe Ruth

LEGENDARY BASEBALL SLUGGER BABE RUTH is most famous for holding a decades-long record for most career home runs scored. What many people don't know is that he was also known as the King of Strikeouts. The Babe had an "all or nothing" style at bat, and he held the record for most strikeouts in the American League five times during his career. His willingness to fail was the key to his success. Visionary Leaders need that same attitude of commitment and steadfastness to change the world and the world of everyone around them. In the words of Ruth himself, "Never let the fear of striking out keep you from playing the game."

Some visionaries are idea-driven, genius inventors full of quirks and idiosyncrasies. Others have deep knowledge in their fields that gives them uncanny insight into the future of their industries. Regardless of leadership style, all visionaries who eventually succeed do so because they have learned from their failures. To the Visionary Leader, adversity and failure are close and familiar friends.

Millions of pages have been written about successful leadership. If you picked up this book looking for a step-by-step instruction manual, I honestly and humbly suggest you look elsewhere. My intention in this book is to offer you my own perspective on Visionary Leadership. My qualifications for doing so are a forty-year career in the healthcare industry, countless hours of self-inquiry, the willingness to put my ideas into words, and the hope that I might inspire others to embrace change.

This book is a collection of the ideas that have created, shaped, and guided my approach to leadership over the last four decades. Much of what I know is part of a unique style that is purely me, just as your style is purely you. This isn't a definitive discussion or a specific roadmap, but rather an anthology of suggestions for you to experiment with. I hope you'll use what I have learned as a fulcrum to leverage change, whether in your organization or within yourself.

You'll see ideas and concepts appear and reappear throughout this book, intertwined with one another in much the same way they are inside my head. Hopefully, a few of them will speak to you. Use the ones that serve you, leave behind the ones that don't. You may find that you are drawn to different sections at different points in your career. While I recommend reading the book straight through the first time around, any one section can provide a dose of inspiration, a moment of contemplation, or a jolt of perspective.

A career is a marvelous journey. If undertaken with courage and curiosity, it produces a life without regret and full of the rewards of happiness and success. In this book, you'll find my journey. If I'm lucky, sharing how I got here may help you get wherever you're headed next.

PART I

THE FUNDAMENTALS OF LEADERSHIP

WHAT IS LEADERSHIP?

"A leader is one who knows the way, goes the way, and shows the way."

—John Maxwell

PEOPLE OFTEN THINK THE QUALITY OF LEADERSHIP is endowed on an individual when he or she graduates from college, receives an MBA from a prestigious university, or lands that first big promotion. Education is vital, and while it certainly helps to have a solid undergraduate degree and a Master's from a well-known school, those are only baby steps in the lifelong journey of becoming a leader. Leadership isn't bestowed upon you by a piece of paper, nor is it guaranteed by following a specific path up the corporate ladder. That's why these efforts often leave people feeling less than satisfied with their careers. I urge you to wipe the slate of your mind clean. Imagine that there are more possibilities than you can possibly comprehend, and that you are free to explore as many as you please.

The potential for leadership exists in all of us. I know that the purists debate whether leaders are born or made, but the reality is that if you are asking that question, you don't understand people.

Leadership is not about a specific style or technique for gaining control. It is about our ability to relate to and influence other people, to help them own and commit to a vision that they accept and then redefine, influenced by their own inner values and belief structures. These belief structures are as unique as your fingerprints: no two sets are exactly alike. The factors that sway each of us are distinctly based on our own personal views of the world. Our motivations for taking action are equally unique, and the endless stream of permutations for individual variables compounds the complexity of leadership.

Leadership comes from within. It is strongest in a person with high self-confidence and a clear sense of purpose. The specifics of that purpose make up a leader's vision. The importance of successfully creating a guiding vision, getting others to buy into the vision, and acting on that vision is the pretext for this book.

To form a vision and bring it to life, you'll need to get used to looking at your world through different lenses. Some of the lenses may frustrate you or be contrary to your perceptions about the way the world "really" works. I will not ask you to change your beliefs in this book, but I do require you to accept the fact that there are different beliefs out there. To be an effective leader, you must honor and respect every mode of thinking and culture that you encounter. If you keep an open mind, you will receive messages from all directions and see things with such clarity that you will be well on your way to understanding Visionary Leadership.

WHAT MAKES
A VISIONARY LEADER?

"Behind every great achievement is a dreamer of great dreams."

—Robert K. Greenleaf

BEFORE WE GET ANY FURTHER, let's define who a Visionary Leader is and what he or she does. For much of this book, I'll be referring to Visionary Leaders in the context of working within an organization. In those circumstances, the Visionary Leader is someone at the top of the executive food chain: Founder, President, or CEO. Highly successful organizations encourage visionary leadership everywhere in the enterprise, keeping in mind that there is only one overriding mission and ultimately one leader. It doesn't make much sense to have an organization full of visionaries acting upon their own unique dreams for the company. Such an organization would have considerable difficulty aligning behind a single mission. What every company does need is one individual at the top who will shape the central mission of the organization and hold it firmly in his or her sights.

What are the duties and responsibilities of the Visionary Leader? This individual's role is to craft and hold a picture of the future of his or her company and possibly even his or her industry. Such a task requires a deep understanding of the field or market, a unique receptivity to new ideas and information, a willingness to push past the status quo, and a penchant for answering questions that have not yet been asked.

The Visionary Leader is not only responsible for creating the vision, he or she is responsible for helping the organization commit to and execute that vision, which involves getting the entire team to adopt the vision as their own. A thorough dedication to achieving the goals and objectives of the organization is paramount. Finally, it is vital that the Visionary Leader can forge relationships and inspire others. Leadership does not exist in a vacuum; it is first and foremost relational to those who are being led.

Although it does not benefit an organization to have each employee working toward his or her own vision for the company, there is still room for leadership on every level. Within a company, each department also needs a Visionary Leader, albeit on a smaller scale, who can run his or her division in accordance to the company's overall mission. Every department needs at least one individual who is intimately acquainted with the unique needs, routines, and personalities involved and is also willing to take responsibility for the department's success.

Imagine your organization full of team members working to improve every department of the company from the inside out. In my field of healthcare, that means leaders in pharmacy, nursing, administration, and custodial staff. How much possibility for success could exist with leaders on all levels working to the singular mission of the organization? The energy, power, and potential are astounding.

There is one other way to define a Visionary Leader that has nothing to do with being the top executive. Regardless of title or position, the tools of this book will apply just as aptly to your life. Each of us is a leader and visionary of our own personal journey. You don't start your leadership journey when you become CEO. You become CEO after you've learned to be the Visionary Leader of your own life.

WHAT DOES A VISIONARY LEADER CONTRIBUTE?

"People don't buy what you do, they buy why you do it."

—Simon Sinek

EARLY IN MY CAREER, I worked for a man who was a true Visionary Leader. He had the gift of being able to look ahead and spent much of his time thinking, trying to discover where his industry was heading next. His sense of imagination and commitment to innovation are characteristics that all true visionaries possess.

Interestingly, this Visionary Leader wasn't hugely successful at the company where we worked. He often did all the wrong things for all the right reasons, and he was never able to fully bring his organization on board with the vision of the future that he saw. This phenomenon led me to examine my own ideas about leadership more closely. What contributions does a Visionary Leader need to make to be successful?

We all know the success stories of our time and the big names associated with them: Bezos & Amazon, Jobs & Apple, Zuckerberg & Facebook. The most successful visionaries don't just see an image of how they want the world to be, they craft a vision and then put it into action with the express goal of benefitting others.

It's not enough to paint a pretty picture for people. If you want to inspire organizations, incite movements, and create lasting, effective change, you must craft a vision that adds value to the world around you. As leadership expert Simon Sinek says, "All the great organizations in the world, all have a sense of why that organization does what it does." This sense of purpose leads to the kind of infectious quality that high-performing companies possess. The ownership felt by employees at every level in a truly inspired organization is palpable, and the enduring quality, performance, and teamwork is noticeable in the results the company achieves. People need to understand and own the vision of their organization, convert that vision into words that make sense for them, and put lasting fingerprints on their personal contributions to the vision. The Visionary Leader's contributions don't begin and end with creating the vision. He or she must be there every step of the way, relentlessly dedicated to moving the vision forward and enlisting every single member of his or her team to join the cause.

LEADERSHIP ISN'T ONE-SIZE-FITS-ALL

"The cornerstone of effective leadership is self-mastery."

—Patricia Aburdene

WHEN YOU HEAR THE WORD LEADER, you probably envision a certain kind of person in your mind. We implicitly identify leaders as charismatic individuals who easily win over the masses. In reality, there is not one stereotype or category that defines, or more importantly predicts, who will become a Visionary Leader. I have seen introverts who are extremely shy and extroverts who are incredibly gregarious both find success. I have met PhDs and high school graduates alike who are great Visionary Leaders for their companies and communities.

Being a strong leader is less about who you are and more about how you adapt to your environment. Some individuals will be incredibly successful in one environment but will fail miserably under a different set of circumstances. I consider a successful leader one who can consistently perform under variable environments and conditions, which is why the ability to adapt and reinvent oneself is a vital aspect of leadership.

"How do I become a leader?" This is a question that many young people, from students to employees, are asking themselves. Most are looking for a silver bullet, a guarantee, a single straight line from here to the top of the organization. The actual path is much more circuitous. To become a good leader is to learn about and transform yourself from the inside out. Just as there is not one leadership style that works for everyone, neither is there one single route that will ensure success.

Although this lack of guaranteed outcome may be discouraging, it also means that anybody can be a leader. You don't need to be born with a certain personality, attend a specific school, or work with the exact "right" mentor to learn leadership. What you must fundamentally understand, however, is that leadership always involves other people. Being a leader is not about you; it's about the impact you have on those around you. The true measure of leadership is not your own success, but the opportunities you create for others to succeed.

Leadership is Learned on the Job, Not in the Classroom

"Education comes from within."

—Napoleon Hill

MANY YOUNG PEOPLE I ENCOUNTER believe they must go through business school to learn leadership and, if they want to be successful, that they need to attend one of the top business schools in the country. A great education from a top tier school can be valuable as the starting point for a career, but academic preparation is only one of many ways to get started on your leadership journey.

Successful leadership is about your ability to create choices and make clear directional changes using all the resources available to you at a given moment in time. Some of these resources will only be accessible if you are open to change. I have always believed that until we are about thirty-five years old, we are students; from thirty-five to forty-five, we are practitioners of our craft; from forty-five to fifty-five, we are teachers; and from fifty-five on, we become teachers of teachers. To be successful we must understand which phase we are in, and in every phase, we must be patient with ourselves and continually practice introspection.

◄O►

My first real lesson about leadership came from a woman named Margarita Shields. I was in graduate school and had a year-long residency at a major university medical center. Mrs. Shields (I would *never* have called her by her first name) was the woman in charge of the night shift. From 11 P.M. – 7 A.M., she played every important role at the hospital: head administrator, Chief Financial Officer, resident chaplain; the list of her responsibilities goes on and on.

As part of my rotation, I was supposed to spend a single night with Mrs. Shields. After shadowing her and observing everything she did over the course of a shift, I extended that night of observation to a full week. I was fascinated by the way this woman brokered the resources and needs of a large medical center. She was effective and efficient beyond measure. During the day, there were probably fifty separate individuals doing the work that she did alone through the nighttime hours.

The most illuminating part was learning that Margarita Shields was a nurse with no formal management training. She excelled at her job because she was so integrated into the inner workings of the hospital; she instinctively knew what needed to happen next. Her knowledge was omniscient and her power was almost unlimited. From 11 P.M. – 7 A.M., she single-handedly ran the medical center like a well-oiled machine.

What I admired most, and tried to learn, was her ability to approach any human being and get them interested and excited about what she needed them to do. Mrs. Shields treated everyone the same, from the housekeeping staff to the physicians. She didn't care about their position or level of seniority; she just cared that they were doing their part to make things run smoothly. She was incredibly skilled in changing her tactics to suit the individual and the situation. Sometimes, all that was required was a look.

Since meeting Mrs. Shields, I've never again thought that formal leadership training was imperative. There are wonderful programs out there that teach important principles of business and leadership, and I am not devaluing those institutions in any way. However, leadership is not primarily learned in the classroom. It is learned when you relate to and work with people, on the job, in the latest hours of the night, when everything is depending on you.

LEADERSHIP REQUIRES BUILDING STRONG RELATIONSHIPS

"In addition to all of the ratios and goals and parameters and bottom lines, it is fundamental that leaders endorse a concept of persons."

—Max DePree

MY EARLY EXPERIENCES IN LEADERSHIP served me well when I became a senior executive in a large hospital management company. We primarily managed not-for-profit hospitals of varying size in both rural and urban areas across twenty-four states. I was responsible for virtually everything west of the Mississippi River. In this role, I realized that relationships are the key to successful business, regardless of location, field of endeavor, scale of the organization, or the role you play within it.

I was living in Dallas at the time, and if one of our hospitals in Colorado or Idaho had a problem at 2 A.M., I couldn't be there in person to put the fire out. My organization's success or failure was determined solely by the quality of my relationships with the administrator of that hospital and the chairperson of its board. If you have great relationships with your clients or customers, you will be forgiven for a lot of mistakes. If you don't have good relationships, you will be punished for the smallest infractions.

Over the last thirty-plus years, I have been fortunate to serve in the highest leadership positions for large health systems which generate over $3,000,000,000 in net revenue and employ over 20,000 team members. Gaining experience on that kind of scale has taught me that strong relationships are a requirement for success in any industry. To be an effective Visionary Leader, you must work constantly on your relationship-building skills.

One critical piece of relationship-building is learning to simplify your communication. When you oversee a large organization, you need to speak in "sound bites", clear, straightforward statements that can reach thousands of employees in a meaningful way. Each employee will process and interpret your strategy and vision for the organization through his or her own lens. This outcome is actually desirable; it's the only way employees will accept and take ownership of the vision for themselves. The goal is for everyone to have "fingerprints" on the vision, and to understand their role in achieving it so clearly that they can (and will) explain it to their relatives or next-door neighbors in a direct and concise manner.

Your vision must be lofty and difficult to achieve, but it should never be confusing. Everyone on your staff needs to understand how their job ties into the overall accomplishments of the organization and what they can do to help the company reach its goals. This process is not easy, so as leaders we must create a set of enduring standards around the vision, as well as provide clear execution steps to get there. Individuals should easily be able to answer the question "What is my role in this vision and how can I contribute to its success?"

In my most recent position, my sound bite was: "The success of any business depends on the relationship between one team member and one patient at a time." I always made it a point to attend new-hire orientations so that our team members heard this message from day one on the job. Even though our employees interacted with thousands of people each day, I encouraged them to see each unique encounter as an opportunity for success or failure. To be a top performer in any industry, you must shoot for 100 percent satisfied customers. Customers are satisfied when they have high-quality relationships with your employees. This requires teamwork and a supportive culture that prioritizes quality, safety, and integrity. Put all that together and you have one of the great keys for success in strong relationships: trust.

Strong relationships are not an end to themselves; they provide the foundation required for significant achievements. Underneath the sound bite "The success of any business depends on the relationship between one team member and one patient at a time" was the most ambitious goal our organization could ever hope to reach: zero-harm healthcare. I knew that zero-harm healthcare, which means that absolutely no patients are harmed by preventable, adverse events while under an organization's care, seemed like such a remote possibility that our team members would find it difficult to rally around the concept. They would feel as though they were always falling short of the goal. I also knew that if we measured our progress by the success one patient encounter at a time, we were laying the groundwork to move toward a zero-harm mindset. A Visionary Leader with a lofty vision must create a complex, integrated set of strategies that, when unified, will accomplish a single goal. At every stage, relationships play a critical role.

Our relationships extend well beyond our businesses. They are the root of family and community life as well. The world is run on relationships, and to be a successful leader you must become masterful at building and sustaining them. Your success is ultimately determined not by what you have learned, but by how well you communicate your knowledge, information, and ideas to other people. The quality of your communication determines whether or not you inspire and influence others to commit to the visions and strategies that you create.

In a world where social media rules the day, where everything is abbreviated and concepts and ideas are detached from actual human interaction, clear, succinct communication is more critical than ever. Workplaces in many industries are still built on person-to-person interactions. Although technical skills and social media savvy are what generate buzz, the often-overlooked human relations component remains integral to a company's success.

It is not your technical skills that will get a team of people to follow you, it is your ability to inspire them to want to achieve your goals. In the words of Margaret Wheatley, "In organizations, real power and energy is generated through relationships. The patterns of relationships and the capacities to form them are more important than tasks, functions, roles and positions." Visionary Leadership is not about how smart people think you are, but how smart you make other people feel.

Building relationships starts with understanding how the people you work with process information and how their thinking is influenced by their personal and unique belief structures. You don't have to change your beliefs, nor should you try to change theirs, but to effectively work with the people in your organization, you must understand each other.

PART II

PREPARING
FOR THE JOURNEY

"Freedom is man's capacity to take a hand in his own development. It is our capacity to mold ourselves."

—Rollo May

TO BECOME A VISIONARY LEADER, you must first spend time working on yourself. There is no shortcut or way around it and the job can't be delegated or outsourced to someone else. It requires boldness and confidence to stand up in front of others, paint a picture of the future, and ask people to help you move toward the image that you've created. The following sections are designed to help you cultivate the mindset of a Visionary Leader, and to embody the important qualities of daring, innovation, resilience, and compassion.

There is no sense worrying about whether you could have started this journey sooner. You'll never know if that would have been possible. You cannot go back and change the past, but you can decide what you will do in this moment, and the next one, and the one after that. Today is not too late. It's exactly the right time.

BE READY—
READY OR NOT

"When the student is ready, the teacher appears."

—Theosophical adage

BEFORE YOU MOVE FORWARD IN YOUR READING, there's one question you need to ask yourself. Be honest about the answer.

"Am I ready?"

If you're trying to maintain the status quo, you aren't ready.

If you're resisting the fact that things are happening differently than you think they should, you're not ready.

If you believe you can control what other people think about you or anything else, you're not ready.

If the answer to the question "Am I ready?" is a resounding no, it's not yet time for you to embrace a new way of thinking. These things need to unfold when the timing is right.

However, if there's a glimmer of possibility in your mind, if you're willing to entertain the idea that there might be another way of perceiving the world, I've got good news:

You're ready.

Readiness matters because your mind must be in a receptive state to undergo transformation or change.

I'll give you an example. Tony Robbins' book *Unlimited Power* has been highly influential in my life, but it's not a read I go around sharing with just anybody. As my daughter became a young woman, I started paying attention to the kinds of conversations we were having together. I heard in her dialogue a thought process that was growing and maturing in a certain way. It made me think she was ready for *Unlimited Power*. I knew it would be a meaningful read for her, and that she'd find a lot of insights that would help her in her career. I also knew that she needed to be ready to receive the information, or the lessons in the book would go unnoticed or ignored.

Did my daughter know she was ready to read *Unlimited Power*? I don't think so. She probably didn't even know it existed. Nor was she aware that I was waiting for the right moment to give her a book that has been so influential on me.

I love the quote "When the student is ready, the teacher appears." You don't always know who the teacher is. It may be somebody who has just entered your life or someone from your past who has unexpectedly reappeared. Or it may be somebody very close, like a father, who suddenly sees you in a different light.

For me, it was my mother's father. A quiet, unassuming Dutchman, he came to the United States in 1903 at the age of sixteen. Although he never had much formal education, my grandfather was undaunted by any adversity and had a perpetually positive attitude. He taught me to look for the good in everything and to never give up. As children, my sister and I would sit with him in his backyard; he would smoke a cigar and tell us stories about his life. One story was about how he and his brothers had a house-moving business in Chicago; while moving a rather large, two-story house across a bridge, the axle on their wagon broke. They worked for two days to lift the house high enough to replace the axle, and in the end, the police made them burn the house, right there on the bridge. We asked him, "What did you do then, Grandpa?"

He replied, "We became farmers."

In life, all of us face moments of self-doubt and uncertainty. Yet, the reality of what we are capable of was demonstrated to me through the undaunted persistence, self-confidence, and proverbial positive attitude of this quiet man who had limited education, but unlimited understanding of the human potential. I learned from him that we are measured only by the limits that we place on our own potential and not by any other external force.

As a Visionary Leader, you cannot predict precisely what teaching you will receive or the way in which those lessons will appear. Your only task is to cultivate openness and receptivity, and to stay awake and alert when opportunities arise.

START
FROM THE INSIDE OUT

"Love everyone unconditionally, including you."

—Ken Keyes

YOU DON'T TAKE A JOURNEY FROM HERE TO THERE; you take a journey from inside to outside yourself. The starting point is always in your mind. There is no goal set, no action taken, no dream achieved that is not initiated by thought. Your journey to happiness, love, success, and independence must start from within.

Just as your journey can only begin inside your mind, likewise, your journey can only begin in the present moment. Setting a starting point in the past means your trip has already begun. A starting point in the future means you have not yet set off on your course. The distance between the beginning of time and yesterday are in the same place: the past. Here and now is the official point of departure if you want to chart a course that is imaginative, unique, and infinite in its possibilities.

My own point of departure was in my late thirties. I had recently been exposed to a lot of New Age content, and I explored Wayne Dyer, Thomas Merton, and James Allen, trying to understand more about consciousness. I wanted to know more about myself and my own motivations.

STEPHEN R. MASON

Like most of us, I had a little voice inside my head. The voice reinforced my thoughts of inadequacy and negative opinions about myself, which kept me continually striving for greater control. I began a process of inward study to find out what was underneath that little voice in my head, and I discovered that to flourish, I would have to learn how to give up control. Through this effort, I gained an understanding of myself and others that catapulted my career and shaped my life in transformative and enduring ways.

When I first experienced this shift, I didn't connect it to the business world. I had made great strides in my own career, but it took quite some time before I connected the reinvention of my consciousness to the reinvention of an organization.

In my forties, I worked for a health system which owned a large insurance company. Nobody knew quite where the healthcare industry was headed, but our CEO went all in on a strategy without the adequate risk assessment or infrastructure needed to support his vision. A series of unpredicted events during this period left us scrambling, and as a result, the organization was faced with a crisis that required a significant change in direction.

One of my responsibilities was to reinvent the relationship between the health system and the insurance company. At the time, there were no roadmaps for this sort of activity. My old instinct would have been to grasp for control and try to force a particular outcome. However, I had been reinventing myself for the last several years, so instead of trying to control the situation, I worked to understand it first. This helped me develop a strategy based on the organization's current resources and capabilities and ultimately, repositioned the organization, leading to a successful turnaround.

At the time, I didn't put together how the shift in my thinking had allowed me to come up with a more creative solution for our company. It eventually became clear to me that I had stepped out of a Type A personality and embraced a sense of not being in control of anything. This fundamental transformation, which started from the inside out, set me free to see new possibilities for bringing an organization to a high-performing state. I was now able to understand the shift occurring in the industry and envision the changes that were occurring. This allowed me to more clearly see the direction that we needed to take. Once I had formed a vision for the desired outcome, I was able to work with my team to create a strategy that involved dozens of tactical moving parts.

UNDERSTAND
THE UNIVERSE

"The universe is not static, but expanding."

—Stephen Hawking

EVERY MOVE WE MAKE IS PART OF THE ORDER OF THE UNIVERSE. Growing a business, scaling an organization, or pivoting a company are not outside of the natural order of the world, but an integral part of its structure. Studying the laws of physics and various theories of the universe has helped simplify highly complex business environments. If you view the universe as being constructed from very small, subatomic particles which are continuously seeking order and a natural state of balance, you gain an appreciation for the potential of high-functioning businesses. They are, after all, called *organizations*.

Stephen Hawking said that our universe is not contracting, not static, but expanding, and he meant it quite literally. The boundaries of the universe are continually pushing outward and have been growing bigger since the universe began. They could continue to expand for billions of years.

In much the same way, the universal consciousness of the world is also continually increasing. Just think about the amount of information that was available before the internet compared to what we have access to today. Our capacity for information has grown exponentially in the last few decades, but it was steadily expanding long before the first computer was built.

If we could raise the self-esteem of everyone on this planet, we would be able to better utilize this expanding consciousness. Humanity would experience a significant growth in knowledge, productivity, and pure potentiality. Nobody would be held back by fear or doubt, and the contributions to our universe and our existence would profoundly increase. By intentionally expanding consciousness to do good, we would encounter new solutions and opportunities, solve our most pressing problems, and create a safer, more united world.

My understanding of our expanding universe has significantly shaped my thinking about consciousness, mindset, and leadership. I once read that at the quantum level, subatomic particles are simultaneously seeking balance and experiencing chaos. This began a period of study on chaos theory, complexity theory, and quantum physics. I was driven by a desire to get to the simplest element, the bottom line on what exactly made up the stuff of the universe. I believed that once I understood how the smallest particles of the universe functioned, I could understand how everything else developed from there.

When you look at a complex situation, try to find the smallest particle possible, the simplest structure within a complicated problem. Getting down to the "subatomic" level helps you identify the root change that must occur for there to be a shift, an answer, or a solution.

Think about what happens when you throw a pebble into a pond. The pebble hits the water and its smooth surface creates ripples, concentric circles that spiral farther and farther away from the center. If you only see the ripples without understanding that they were made by the pebble, you're privy to the effect, but are fundamentally missing the cause.

You must understand both the pebble and its trajectory to create effective change. Grounding yourself in this simplicity allows you to examine and build layers of complexity without getting overwhelmed. When you understand things at the subatomic level, you can readily identify the particulars of a situation: how many people you need in what kind of organizational structure, what new jobs and activities you need to create, and what resources or skills are required to make it all happen.

RECOGNIZE THE ILLUSION OF CONTROL

"You may not control all the events that happen to you, but you can decide not to be reduced by them."

—Maya Angelou

IF YOU WANT TO BE SUCCESSFUL, one of the most important shifts you can make is to give up the illusion of control. We spend so much energy each day imagining we have control: of our own thoughts, of other people, of our environment, of the world at large.

Our brains are wired to believe that the patterns of the past will determine the future; in many ways, this is an important survival mechanism. It seems certain that the sun will rise each morning and that gravity will continue to be a force in nature, but there is no way to know this for sure. We make similar assumptions about our relationships, our careers, and even our health. We take for granted that the coffee shop around the corner will always be open, until one day, the doors are shuttered. We presume that our jobs are safe, until we find ourselves in an industry struggling to redefine itself to be sustainable for the future. The reality is that we have absolutely no way of predicting what will happen from one moment to the next.

Trying to predict what happens next is a means of grasping for control. For many, life seems inconceivable and unmanageable without this story.

Letting go of control can be incredibly difficult, as it involves embracing the inherent uncertainty life must offer. Organizations often struggle with giving up control because they don't have experience in what the future seems to require. Examples across history, from the manufacturing of gas street lamps to Blockbuster's failure to jump into the digital media game, illustrate the potential for catastrophic results when we refuse to relinquish control.

What you must understand is that you're only letting go of the *illusion* of control. You were never actually in control of anything in the first place.

Releasing the illusion of control is a form of surrender, and when you surrender, you stop worrying about all the things that were troubling you before. You stop limiting yourself based on your past, because the uncertainty of the next moment means that anything can happen, and there are no boundaries on what you are able to accomplish. You stop pushing so hard to achieve a guaranteed outcome, because you understand that there are no real guarantees. Letting go of the illusion of control allows you to be more aware of the world around you and to receive messages and information that have been waiting to guide you all along.

Most of what isn't working for you in your life is a direct result of your own actions. In striving for control, you limit your abilities and sabotage your own success. This stems from a mindset of scarcity, needing to control and keep whatever it is you have, whether that's love, money, or status. The underlying belief is that there is only so much of these things to go around, and that we must all fight tooth and nail to retain what we've got.

Remember how the universe is continually expanding? It's a generous universe in the sense that there is always more being created. It's a space of abundance if you are willing to claim that generosity. At the same time, you must recognize that you are not in charge of the universe. The universe is neutral and inherently disinterested in your charade of control. It is moving on, and whether you choose to acknowledge its expansion or not, the universe is taking you along for the ride.

The actual mechanism that underlies our need for control is the link between our conscious and subconscious minds. Think about the external stimulation that you are getting in the space where you are right now. There are literally thousands of contact elements that are bombarding your conscious mind: colors, sounds, thoughts, and more. So much stimulation would drive you crazy if it wasn't buffered in some form, and that is where the subconscious mind gets involved. Your brain intentionally limits the number of stimuli that your conscious mind can focus on in any given moment. For this to occur, your subconscious mind acts as a filter, limiting the content your conscious mind receives. This allows you to focus and think clearly about a small number of things at once.

How does the subconscious mind choose the material that it screens and sends to the conscious mind? That determination is a result of the input that you intentionally provide. In the words of James Allen, "We become what we think about all the time." Understanding this concept is vital to becoming a Visionary Leader. Change what you are thinking about, and you will start seeing answers to questions that you never saw before. The solutions and the information were always there, but now your subconscious mind is buffering them into your conscious mind.

Here's a classic example: you go car shopping and end up buying a new, red SUV. As you're driving your car home, you're amazed by how many other red SUVs are out on the road. The make, model, color, even the year of your car are identical. Everywhere you go, you notice these red SUVs: at the gas station, on the highway, even in your neighborhood. It's as though the whole world just went out and bought red SUVs too.

What's really going on here? It's not likely that the sales of your particular red SUV have suddenly spiked. It's simply that your subconscious mind was previously filtering out the red cars. Now that you own one yourself, that information is getting through to your conscious mind. Hence, you see red SUVs everywhere you go.

Once you release yourself from the illusion of control, every encounter has the potential to help you achieve your vision. When a friend calls me to say I should really go to lunch with his friend because we'd have a lot to talk about, I usually accept the invitation. I am interested in the possibility of what I might discover, and I take it as a sign of sorts that my friend thought to put the two of us together in the first place. When I was "in control", I might have ignored the opportunity if I didn't see the immediate connection to my career or my organization. I would have missed the opportunity to find out where the encounter could take me.

When you are open to possibility and expansion, you may find that these opportunities lead to something valuable in support of your vision. Your perspective changes when you are no longer under the pressure of the control illusion. Even if the ideas you're introduced to don't seem to fit your vision or align with your understanding of the current environment, you're wise to store the idea rather than discard it. Years later, the information you gained may become invaluable.

By steering your mind from the inside out and not being driven by pre-defined, external stimuli, you reposition the priority that you place on information. Your subconscious mind begins to capture and filter data that will provide support for the vision that you constantly think about. You focus on perfecting the vision in your mind rather than assessing the value of the information you are continually gaining. Let your subconscious store that data and determine its future usefulness when the time comes.

To recognize the illusion of control is to liberate your mind. You may have leadership abilities that you previously did not believe you possessed. In an expanding universe, there are many great ideas that have not yet been discovered. Rather than limit your growth by grasping for control, let go of the illusion and begin tapping into your true potential.

STOP THE DANCE
OF SELF-DOUBT

"Heroes are ordinary people who have achieved extraordinary things in life."

—David Winfield

WHEN YOU LET THE VOICE INSIDE YOUR HEAD—the one critiquing you, worrying about what other people think, constantly trying to protect you from failure—pull your strings, you are like a puppet caught in the dance of self-doubt. Stopping the dance is much harder than it sounds. Thousands of personal development books have been written about self-discovery and self-healing, but quieting the voice inside our heads often feels like an insurmountable challenge.

The only real way to stop the dance of self-doubt is to learn how to stand still. When you notice yourself caught up in the dance, slow down. Stop, if only for a moment. Be patient with yourself. Start over as many times as you need to (and you will need to start over many times). Eventually, you will be able to stop the dance of self-doubt even before the music begins.

Being caught in the dance of self-doubt doesn't mean there is anything wrong with you. In fact, it's an indication that you are 100 percent human. The truth is that the world is run by imperfect individuals who test their own limits and accomplish great things. Why let anything about yourself be a limitation? You can break the cycle any given day, any given moment, even this one.

DEFINE YOURSELF

"No one can make you feel inferior without your consent."

—Eleanor Roosevelt

WE FACE SIGNIFICANT CHALLENGES and take hits to our egos every single day. Rather than letting yourself be defined by your responses to these external forces, it's important to develop an internal sense of yourself to guide you.

You have a unique opportunity to define the principles and values that make up what I call "the logic of me". It begins with the question "Who am I?" and ends with the realization that you alone are responsible for coming up with the answer.

No one else can—or should—be allowed to define you. It's your job to clearly define yourself and to be comfortable with who you are, particularly if you're going to lead a group of people. Make no mistake, if you don't clearly define yourself, others will try to do it for you.

It's like driving a car that you've had for years. You understand the limits of its performance: how fast it can go, how far it can travel on a tank of gas, how it handles in the rain.

How well do you understand your mind? Do you know where you perform well and where you don't? If you can reach the point where you truly understand yourself, the next step is to recognize you have the power to change the course of your life, to ensure that you are never defined by someone else's ideals again.

ASK, "WHAT IF YOU COULDN'T FAIL?"

"While much has been said about fear of failure,
it still is the single biggest obstacles people face
to creative success."

—Tom Kelley

WHAT WOULD YOU DO if you knew that you absolutely could not fail? If success was guaranteed, what bold actions would you dare to take? How might you live your life differently each day? Which goals and expectations would you set just a little higher?

When I ask this question to kindergarteners, they answer without hesitation. They will be firemen, astronauts, ballet dancers, doctors, and teachers. They don't lower their standards, make practical selections, or create backup plans.

When I ask middle schoolers this same question, however, the responses are quite different. They are immediately suspicious. "What do you mean, guaranteed not to fail? How could you know that for sure?" At twelve years old, they might say, "Well, I wanted to be an astronaut when I was a kid." By the time we are pre-teens, we have started to lose our innocence. Doubt has crept in, and we question whether we are good enough, smart enough, or strong enough. We no longer believe that we can be anything we want to be.

It's even harder to let our imaginations run wild as we grow up. We are continually sabotaging our own success because of that little voice in our head—the one which has been reinforced by parents, teachers, bosses, and bullies—that limits our ability to express our full potential.

You don't have to believe that you can't fail, at least not yet. You do have to be willing to ask yourself the question "What would I do if I knew I couldn't fail?" The answers might surprise or even scare you. However, I guarantee that the responses your mind provides can guide you, if you're willing, to undertake a deeper exploration of yourself and a more courageous way of living.

FORGET THE QUESTION AND LET THE ANSWER APPEAR

"We shall not cease from exploration / And the end of all our exploring / Will be to arrive where we started / And know the place for the first time."

—T.S. Eliot

YOUR MIND IS AN AMAZING INSTRUMENT which operates with computer-like precision. Your brain remembers and stores everything that you observe. The challenge is to be able to retrieve that stored information when you need it. The conscious effort of trying to force your mind to produce solutions is often stress-inducing and unproductive. Counterintuitive though it may be, calming your thought process and releasing your grip on control is more likely to bring forth the answer you are seeking.

The relationship between the conscious and subconscious mind, discussed in an earlier chapter, is the key to unlocking the brain's vault of information. If the subconscious mind filters the data that the conscious mind receives, then you can use this preexisting pathway to effectively come up with solutions. In other words, ask your mind the right questions and allow the answers to appear.

Think back to a time when something occurred to you, but you couldn't remember where you learned the information. Or a time when the solution to your problem suddenly became so clear that it seemed as though the answer was there all along. These strange phenomena are part of the mind's process of storing and utilizing information based on your current circumstances.

Quieting your mind is an important part of this process. I think of it as creating space for the right information to break through. Later in this book, I talk about the practice of meditation. Learning to meditate will help you clear your thoughts and calm your mind. Once your mind is clear, ask yourself in a positive way the questions that you would like answered. Then, simply forget about the questions and trust that your mind will go to work producing the answers you are looking for. It may take several hours or days for the answers to appear, but your next best step will arrive, if not the entire solution to your problem. Practice this technique frequently for best results.

MASTER THE INFINITE SIX INCHES OF SPACE BETWEEN YOUR EARS

"Circumstance does not define the person, it reveals them."

—James Allen

THE DIAMETER OF THE AVERAGE HUMAN CRANIUM is approximately six inches.[1] Roughly the same diameter as a cantaloupe, this is, in fact, the vastest area in the universe. The infinite space between your ears is the source of all ideas, all knowledge, and all perspective you bring to the world. Within your own infinite six inches of space, you have the chance to decide how to face life's challenges. Whether you are joyful or sorrowful, grateful or bitter, carefree or burdened is purely dependent on the attitude you choose. You have the ability to change that attitude in an instant.

Will today be miserable or glorious? The answer is simple. If you are lucky enough to wake up and ask the question, you get to decide. The expanding universe of your mind is where the choice is made. If there is anything in life you can control, it may be the way you choose to perceive the world. Your perspective tends to be a self-fulfilling prophecy. This could be the most miserable day of your life—if you choose to believe it is. It could also be the most glorious. Your experience is completely up to you. If that

---

[1] https://www.bwc.ohio.gov/downloads/blankpdf/ErgoAnthropometricData.pdf

responsibility seems daunting, remember that you can change your attitude in an instant. The mind is highly sensitive to suggestion, and it only takes a moment to flip your perspective 180 degrees.

Despite this incredible power, many of us remain paralyzed by self-doubt and fear. Perhaps it is precisely because we are so powerful that we feel unable to act. Acknowledging the force that you wield would make you accountable for the way you move through life. Instead, you start listening to that little voice in our head, which is reinforced by the conditioning of well-meaning parents, teachers, and friends, as well as the injuries to your self-esteem from rivals and enemies. When you do so, you fail to realize that it is you, and not your circumstances, that create the conditions of your existence. If you believe the world is out to get you, for example, your subconscious mind will filter through information and examples that reinforce that belief.

For visionaries who want to cultivate an effective leadership style, what's going on between your ears is critical in determining the kind of leader you will become. Leaders whose internal self-talk is a constant stream of negative criticism will have difficulty confidently sharing their ideas, soliciting honest feedback, and relinquishing control. On the other hand, leaders who consciously change their self-talk and tell themselves a different story about what they're capable of can achieve much more, and with far greater support, than they might have imagined.

Learn from the Twelve-Step Process

*"I've had many problems in my life - most of which
never happened."*

—Mark Twain

HAVE YOU EVER THOUGHT TO YOURSELF, "If I knew back then what I know now, how much further along the path might I be?" It is common for self-discovery to bring with it a sense of regret, for years of needless suffering, for living in the dark, for struggling through the forest when the path was nearby. However, one of life's great lessons is that it is never too early and never too late to start the journey of self-discovery. In fact, the only time you can begin is now, and now is exactly the right time for you to begin.

I mentioned in an earlier chapter that I started my personal journey when I was in my thirties, reading the works of writers such as Wayne Dyer and James Allen. Another tool I found valuable during this time was the Twelve Steps used by Alcoholics Anonymous. Even though I have never been addicted to drugs or alcohol, I found that I could still apply pieces of the process to create self-transformation.

One of the things I learned was how to clear away the weight of my excess emotional baggage. Like most of us, I had collected my fair share of doubt, anger, disappointment, and resentment over the years. By holding onto insults or slights from my past, as long ago as my childhood, I was holding myself back from realizing my full potential as an adult. We all have examples where somebody made us feel we weren't good enough, a feeling we believed and internalized far beyond the point where it was motivational or helpful.

Using the Twelve Steps as a loose roadmap, I took inventory of all that useless baggage, forgave others for things they had done to hurt me, and asked others to forgive me where I had done the same. I found this incredibly liberating. It stripped away all my excuses about why I was the way I was and forced me to bear responsibility for my own emotional state. It is always easier to place blame on someone or something other than yourself, but when I took charge of my own feelings, I recognized that the only person who could make me feel angry, hurt, or disappointed was me. The ability to authentically and honestly examine your own feelings and failings is imperative on the journey of self-discovery.

SERVE TWO SCOOPS
OF SELF-ESTEEM

*"(A manager) once confided in me she liked to picture in
her mind's eye that every employee was wearing one of
those sandwich billboard signs. On the front side, the
sign would read 'Appreciate Me' and on the back side
'Make me Feel Important'"*

—James Hunter

WHEN YOU HAVE LOW SELF-ESTEEM, you tend to see the universe as contracting
rather than expanding. You feel there is not enough to go around, and you
cling to and protect what little you do have. That's the product of limiting
beliefs, reinforced by the voice inside your head. When that voice starts to
enumerate the list of reasons why you're not good enough, it's time to stop
the dance of self-doubt. If you look in the mirror and are unable to love the
person you see, you'll find it extremely difficult to achieve your potential.

How much further along would we all be if we instead adopted the perspective that there are no limits to who we are and what we can accomplish?
Imagine what the world would be like if we could give everyone two scoops
of self-esteem each day. With high, healthy self-confidence, we would be
more productive, more creative, more imaginative, and more generous. We
could significantly raise our collective consciousness.

How do you give yourself self-esteem? It essentially comes down to making the choice to believe in yourself and let go of your limiting thoughts. Each new moment presents an opportunity to make a change, and that change only takes an instant. Remember that the only thing you can actually control is how you respond to your circumstances. The choice is always yours, as is the responsibility for the choice you make. The more you condition your brain to understand your power in this regard, the better off you will be.

Once you have begun to boost your own self-esteem, the next step is to boost the self-esteem of the people around you. It's critical that you start from the inside out here; to authentically engage with other people, you must first be comfortable with yourself. However, as a Visionary Leader, it is your responsibility to bring your ideas and unique gifts back into the world. That means creating opportunities for others to improve their own self-esteem. Incidentally, a team in which every individual is confident and has healthy self-esteem makes for the best work force you could possibly imagine.

I'll give you two simple ways to build self-esteem in others:

1   Do the inner work on your own self-esteem. Be a model of
    the self-confidence you want others to feel.
2   Greet everyone you encounter with a kind word and a smile.

I am sometimes asked, "Why would I tell someone they are doing a great job for doing the work I pay them to do?" This question shows a fundamental lack of understanding about the way people work. Human beings are powered by self-esteem, so it's not only nice to tell everyone you meet that they are doing a great job, it's vital. Imagine how you would feel if you were mopping a floor and everyone who walked by remarked on what a great job you were doing. That single act could provide an entire week's worth of high self-esteem, and your sense of motivation and pride in your work would increase exponentially. Now, multiply that self-esteem across every member of your organization and imagine the potential for growth.

Self-esteem creates respect and love for yourself. As a Visionary Leader, you need to cultivate respect and self-love in others as well. You must do for other people what you do for yourself. When other people feel good, they'll find success, support others, and keep the cycle going. This contributes to the expansion of the universe, making it a place of generosity and abundance rather than of scarcity and want.

Most people can only get 85 percent of the way on their own. The plagues of self-doubt and a lack of confidence prevent them from tapping into their infinite potential. Your job is to help the people around you replicate the same growth you have found within yourself. This will not make you weak nor will it make you vulnerable. Rather, self-esteem elevates and expands the capability of organizations, strengthens the culture, and enables others to align their personal vision with the vision of the organization.

If you successfully involve and inspire others, you can bring them on board with you. Be bold and open about the changes you propose to make. If you want to be successful, you need to be prepared to do something risky. If you have continually boosted your own self-esteem and the confidence of those around you, you will have inspired their trust. They will be willing to listen and understand the vision of where you, and they, are headed next.

Building self-esteem is a cyclical process that is repeated over and over again. Every individual in the Cycle of Self-Esteem will improve not only his or her own life, but the lives of others as well.

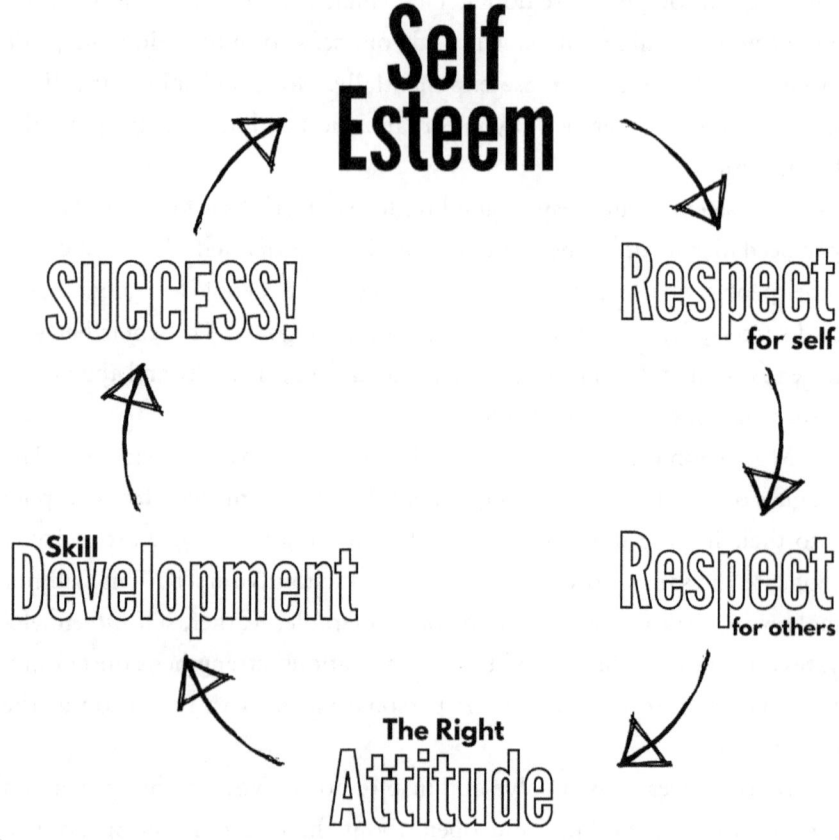

It all starts with being able to manage that little voice inside your head. It is unlikely that you will ever be able to silence it completely, so instead, put your inner voice to work for you. Remember that this voice is connected to your subconscious mind, which is helping you to become what you think about all the time. Imagine that you have harnessed the voice to only tell you positive things, and to reinforce the vision that you have crafted for yourself. With this kind of reinforcement, you can significantly reduce your stress and your suffering and become what you choose to be.

The key is to be patient with yourself. As you start redirecting the little voice in your head, you will inevitably have periods where you regress. Old habits and fears will come back. Rather than struggling and resisting the voice, pause for a moment. Address the negative thought head-on and then redirect your thinking. This is a process of reformation, not removal. Come to grips with the fact that you are a novice at giving up the need for control. Commit to the process of patiently redirecting your thinking and you will achieve a state where all your thoughts and actions are unified around and cooperating harmoniously with the vision you are striving to achieve.

As you build your own self-esteem, your ego will be less fragile. As a result, you'll gain a deeper appreciation for the thoughts, ideas, and observations of others, and see how they are contributing to the successes you achieve. Most importantly, you will find that the voice inside your head has stopped being your harshest critic and started to become your most trusted advisor.

FIND YOUR PERSONAL BALANCE POINT

"Action expresses priorities."

—Mahatma Gandhi

YOU ARE AN ECOSYSTEM UNTO YOURSELF and simultaneously part of many other ecosystems: your body, your family, your organization, your community. Each of these ecosystems is continually seeking balance, just like the tiniest particles of the universe. Balance is subjective, dependent on which system you are considering, and is a continually moving target. Sometimes, you need to be more of a parent; other days more a CEO, activist, worshipper, or friend. Finding balance within the ecosystem of yourself allows you to make more meaningful contributions to the other systems of which you are an integral part.

You can have a fulfilling personal life and a thriving career at the same time, provided that you understand how to use your time well in accordance with your priorities. Striking the balance between professional and personal at any given phase of your life is no easy feat, which is why it's important to come up with a clear plan of how those pieces of your life will work together. It takes work and cooperation with other parties (bosses, spouses, family members, and even friends), but success can be achieved.

Whenever I want to categorize my priorities, I turn to one of my favorite visioning tools: the mind map.

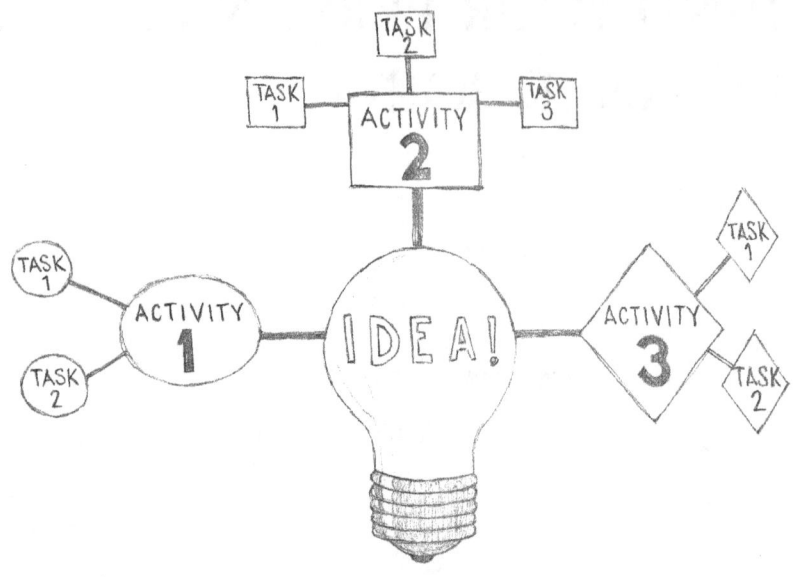

To create a mind map, take a blank sheet of paper and draw a circle in the center of it. Write your ultimate goal or vision inside the circle. Next, draw another series of circles, each connecting to the original circle, until you have identified all the conflicting and related responsibilities and activities in your life. From each of the secondary circles, draw lines out to subsidiary circles that relate to or are dependent on the secondary circle. The secondary or subsidiary circles may be family, hobbies, church, other part-time job, or education, to use a few examples. The next step is to think about time allocation and importance relative to the goal in the center. Is each activity necessary, and does it take you toward your goal or farther from it?

You want to edit and reevaluate your mind map on a regular basis. For example, your goal may be to become a C-suite executive, and your outer circles might be family, graduate program, sailing, golf, blogging, and church activities. When you and your spouse were first married, it may have been easy to balance all the circles, but when the first child came along or your job started to require more traveling, the ability to accomplish the activities in all the circles probably became a challenge. Change is inevitable, so you must be willing and even plan to adjust the map of your life. Now that you've let go of the illusion of control, adjusting your attitude and tweaking your plan are your primary points of leverage.

Your definition of success should always be based on your own personal vision for your life. Ask yourself what you want to do. If you allow your plan to evolve based on the opportunities that come your way, you will be surprised at what you can achieve. Use perspective to manage your expectations. Stay focused and adjust your mind map as often as you need to enjoy the life that you are already living while moving toward future goals. Let your own personal ecosystem guide you. If you find yourself unhappy, your mind is telling you that your personal ecosystem is not in balance. Resist old habits of letting that voice in your head beat on your self-esteem; revisit your plan and be willing to do whatever it takes to accomplish your goals. Acknowledge life for the exciting adventure that it is, and you'll be able to find joy on the path to success.

REDUCE STRESS

*"Do not anticipate trouble or worry about what may
never happen. Keep in the sunlight."*

—Marcus Aurelius

I ONCE READ that only about 7 percent of the things we worry about are
worth the worry. This 7 percent includes the life-threatening or life-changing
issues that we should be focused on reducing, eliminating, or dealing with
to limit their impact on our lives. The other 93 percent are either inconse-
quential concerns or events that will never happen.

Most stress is a product of a malfunctioning mindset, which means you
must handle it from the inside out. When you feel stressed, try to identify the
root cause of your concern. Stress is a symptom or manifestation of a deeper
problem, but the root cause may not be obvious at first glance. To solve a
problem, you must first be able to define it. Ask yourself whether your stress
is a product of external factors or whether it is self-imposed. Even most stressors that seem to be caused by external factors are aggravated by the thoughts
and ideas you add inside your head. In other words, you may well face situations that are stressful, but your mind tends to add fuel to the fire.

Stress is not only detrimental to the creative process and self-confidence;
it also negatively impacts your physical health in a big way. Cardiovascular

disease, weight gain, and depression are all exacerbated by stress. Stress is one of the greatest ills of our society and is constantly placed on people in unnecessary ways, usually as a product of unreasonable expectations. Take, for example, children who are put into intensive academic programs and, as elementary schoolers, end up with several hours of homework each night. Incidentally, if you are a parent who believes pushing your child now will bring him or her happiness later, keep in mind that some of the happiest people in the world have very little in terms of material wealth or possessions.

One of the simplest ways to reduce stress is to recognize the illusion of control. Once you recognize that you are truly not in control, you can clearly see that nobody else is either. If you give up your desire to control the situations and people around you, you'll find you are naturally a lot more relaxed. Even the stressors that are worth worrying about are beyond the reach of what you can control. Adversity will come your way, but it is not an impenetrable barrier to success.

KEEP YOURSELF
IN PERSPECTIVE

"Pride makes us artificial and humility makes us real."

—Thomas Merton

WE ALL OUGHT TO BE LIFELONG STUDENTS, but sometimes, it seems the younger you are, the less you think you need the advice of others. If you overreach or try to take on roles you are not quite ready for, you may be setting yourself up for failure.

I was recently speaking with a colleague who had just finished evaluating a young man in his organization. This guy, who was quite talented, felt that he was ready to be a Vice President in his organization and wanted to know when he would have the opportunity to move up. My colleague was in the unfortunate position of informing him that even though he had great potential, he wasn't yet performing at a VP level. The young man could not understand this response and was upset over the idea that he would have to wait and gain more experience before being eligible for a promotion.

There are some skills that can only be honed over time, and it's important to keep yourself in perspective. Unless you're a professional athlete, don't expect to be at the top of your field before age thirty-five. You're still a student until then. Yes, you may be displaying rapid growth, but there is a natural maturation process that occurs as you get older. Even the most tremendous effort won't speed up the passage of time. It's not worth sacrificing the experiences you need to excel in your career to reach your goals more quickly. Enjoy the opportunity to be in a learning environment and soak up all the knowledge and expertise you can.

Always think of the first day of a new job as the first day of the job that you are going to create for yourself. Every successful person that I know or have studied has followed this path. The idea that you get a promotion first and then develop the skills required for your new role is backward. First, demonstrate that you can perform at a higher level; that will get you noticed and the promotion will follow. Never be too eager to exceed your level of competency. Trying to force acceleration will only slow you down.

I suggest you let your career float, especially when you're young. Don't stay in a job because you feel the need to hold a certain title in a certain amount of time. Opportunity often knocks when you least expect, and in some cases, from the least likely directions and people possible. In my own career, I usually got the chance to move forward when I had prepared myself to make a change. Rather than fighting to meet an arbitrary standard of success, work toward developing a series of skills and set goals that position you for career advancement, and you will embody the qualities that get you noticed and help you advance.

When young people ask me for job advice, I always recommend looking at four key criteria, in this order:

1   The person who you will work for.
2   The organization you are joining.
3   The scope of the job itself.
4   What the position pays.

While it is common to focus on what a position pays as the most important criterion, the person you are working for is actually the factor that matters most. The old saying goes, "People leave managers, not companies." In other words, people usually leave their jobs because they don't like the person who they are working for. A bad manager can make any position thoroughly unenjoyable, while a good boss can act as a mentor to impart significant knowledge and wisdom in addition to creating a pleasant work environment that promotes development and growth.

The next most important criterion is the organization you are joining. You want to go to work in an organization that has a great culture and where you feel valued. The third most important is the job itself. You want plenty of flexibility to expand your skills and create the growth potential that you will need to get to the next level. Finally, pay is in fact the least important of these four considerations. Choose your path based on who you're working for, the organization you're joining, and the job itself, and allow the money to follow.

AVOID THE PITFALLS
OF WORKAHOLISM

*"Never get so busy living that you forget to make
a life."*

—Dolly Parton

A GREAT MANY LEADERS—and many great leaders—struggle with control. The Type A personalities, the workaholics, the micromanagers: they all wrestle with giving up the illusion of control. Although I talked about giving up control in an earlier chapter of the book, I'll warn you that reading a few pages of theory is unlikely to solve your control issues for good. The need for control is strong and requires constant vigilance to keep it in check. Individuals who can't give up the illusion of control need to be involved in or in charge of everything. As leaders, this leaves them depleted and fatigued, isolates them from their teams and support systems, and cuts dramatically into their personal time.

I can sympathize with readers who feel like they can't catch up and therefore believe they must work increasingly harder to try to get ahead. I was a workaholic myself for many years.

My mind was constantly at the office, and my personal ecosystem was out of balance. At the time, I was working about twelve hours a day. At one point, I started to scrutinize my daily schedule, and I noticed something interesting. I was doing a whole lot of unnecessary things just to fill up those twelve hours, creating priorities and adding items to my to-do list that weren't vital to the core responsibilities of my job. So, I stopped doing them. I eliminated any extraneous activities and cut back to an eight-hour workday. Something miraculous happened when I did. My job performance didn't suffer at all. Working less, doing less, it all seemed to get done anyway.

The self-discovery processes I've laid out in these chapters are what finally allowed me to let go of my need for control and the constant sense that I should be doing more. Once I came out on the other side, I noticed something interesting about workaholics. Although they work hard, most of them are still discontented with their careers. More work doesn't bring them more happiness; in fact, the correlation seems to work exactly opposite of the way you'd expect it to.

It's admirable to be passionate about one's career, particularly if you're a Visionary Leader at the helm of an organization. That said, there are too many people who use their careers as placeholders for other areas in their lives where they lack fulfillment or satisfaction. By refusing to examine those other areas and continuing to fill their days with work, they are all but guaranteeing that they will never reach their full potential.

If you're unwilling to give up your mindset of control, keep in mind: as long as you buy into the illusion of control, you'll never achieve all that's possible for you. At the end of the day, you won't be as happy as you could have been either. If you've recognized yourself as a Type A workaholic, read these sections closely and let them sink in. Then, go back and revisit the chapter titled "Recognize the illusion of control."

Cross off what's unnecessary on your to-do list. Surround yourself with good people and trust that they know how to help you, often better than you can yourself! Create clear boundaries between your work and home lives and adhere to them consistently. This will ground you, and help you become a clear model for your organization and its employees.

In the evenings and on the weekends, I typically don't bring my work home with me. It's my time to rest from thinking about things, or at the very least, to let my conscious mind have a break while my subconscious mind works out solutions.

Of course, this doesn't mean that as a CEO, I closed shop promptly at 5 P.M. every day. Sometimes, despite my best efforts, there were demands on my attention that required me to work late. At a certain point in my career, I decided I would rather occasionally stay later at the office to finish my work than come home and feel my attention was divided. Whenever I ran late, I made sure to communicate that to the relevant parties (my wife), along with an explanation. I didn't make a regular habit of it.

When you're home, you're there for quality time, whether that's with your spouse, your kids, or your pet parakeet. Your physical presence is not enough; you need to be present mentally and emotionally as well. It's your choices that determine whether your home environment is a peaceful retreat from work or an extension of your office life. If home isn't a peaceful retreat, I recommend you examine that seriously and take the steps required to make a change.

Email is one of the few exceptions to my rule about taking work home over the weekend. Just about any member of a large organization understands the tremendous amount of email that quickly piles up in your inbox. You can spend hours just sifting and sorting, trying to determine what's important and requires your response.

Sometimes, on a Sunday morning, when the rest of the family was still asleep, I would sit down for an hour or two and knock out a bunch of emails. It was convenient for me, I loved starting the week prepared rather than behind, and I could work without cutting into quality time with family.

At a certain point, however, I recognized that as the CEO, sending emails on a Sunday morning has consequences. When a Vice President receives an email on a Sunday morning from the CEO, he or she might feel the need to respond immediately. So, I try to be sensitive to how others in my organization tend to respond and to communicate where possible that my emails don't constitute an emergency. I'd much rather my team members also enjoy their Sunday mornings instead of spending time writing me back.

What's the essential motivator that's driving all workaholics? It's fear. Fear that they're not good enough, fear that they will fail, fear of letting down their loved ones.

I have good news and bad news for you.

The bad news is that at some point, you will probably fail. There is even a high likelihood that at some point, you will be fired. That's just life. Failing at something doesn't mean you are a failure as a person.

The good news is: it's never the only job you're going to get.

Most people who get fired find a new position that is equally good as or better than the one they had before. Yet, a huge number of people stay in jobs where they are dissatisfied, or don't speak up about what they need, or where they are overworked, because they are afraid of being let go. It's never the only job you're going to get.

You never need to feel like you must stay in a position where you are not moving toward your personal vision of the future. Change can be intimidating, but diving into the realm of "what we don't know that we don't know" also brings a host of new and exciting opportunities.

STOP THE INSANITY AND EMBRACE IMAGINATION

"The definition of insanity is doing the same thing repeatedly and expecting different results."

—att. Albert Einstein

THERE IS AN ALL-TOO-HUMAN TENDENCY to not recognize that the results we get are inextricably linked to the processes we use to achieve them. To change the outcome, we must be willing to try a different approach. If we can change our frame of reference and how we think about a problem, we have the potential to change how we behave. This shift can dramatically alter our results, and it's what has led to one scientific breakthrough after another.

Once you've created your vision, you must be able to communicate it to others. If you are not rallying your employees to your side in the way you hoped, it's time to change your strategy for reaching them. If you are not seeing the progress and growth that you anticipated, you must reassess your methods and processes to see effective change. Otherwise, you're enacting the definition of insanity.

Working in the healthcare industry, I often heard that the system was "broken". The reality is that the payment model for healthcare is designed to get exactly the results we've been getting for the last fifty-plus years. The problem is that half a century later, we want a different set of results. Many health systems are trying to keep the current payment model intact while hoping for a different outcome despite evidence that continuing to operate this way will ultimately lead to failure of the entire industry. This, of course, is the definition of insanity. The product life cycle of the current payment model is unsustainable for the future of healthcare. We must overhaul the model entirely if we want to see meaningfully different results that can carry us into the next century.

If the healthcare industry fails, it will be because it has refused to adapt and continued to cling to the status quo. It's difficult to shift the way we do things because we base our present actions on our past experiences. Those experiences inform our beliefs about how our industries, our relationships, and our careers "should" operate. When we see evidence that the model is not working the way it used to, our world is shaken. We don't know how to reshape our beliefs.

It is far more intimidating to rely on your own imagination to show you what's possible, yet that is exactly what a Visionary Leader must be able to do. Einstein's antidote to the insanity of repeating our mistakes over and over again was to harness the power of imagination:

> *"Imagination is more important than knowledge. For knowledge is limited to all we now know and understand, while imagination embraces the entire world, and all there ever will be to know and understand."*
>
> —Albert Einstein

Imagination is a playground of the mind. It has created the world's biggest breakthroughs in technology and its greatest works of art. Cultivating and expanding your imagination should be one of your most treasured goals.

The tiny ecosystem inside your brain is every bit as infinite as the limitless universe that surrounds you. A single imagination has the same potential for expansion and growth as the universe. The way technology has blossomed and boomed in the last few decades is amazing. In the healthcare industry alone, the technology that's on the horizon will truly blow your mind.

A Visionary Leader must use imagination to explore different ways of approaching a problem. This leads to a greater likelihood of hitting upon the best solution. If you get stuck in the box of routine, status quo, and "the way things have always been done", it's hard to make real inroads of innovation. Yet, it is innately human to try to maintain the status quo.

When the pressure to change becomes strong enough, people shift. The problem with waiting until the water boils, so to speak, on an organizational level is that it's often too late to implement meaningful infrastructure that supports change in a positive direction. Sometimes, change means that things fall apart.

You can't know in advance whether your carefully structured plans will be successful. What you can know is that you have a greater opportunity to make an impact because you were willing to color outside of the lines, to break the mold of the way things have always been done, and even to be completely wrong. If you want a different result, you must change the way you try to get there. The only guarantee is that what you're doing now will maintain the status quo. Everything you're currently doing is designed to get the results that you are getting. If you want a different result, use your imagination to come up with a different approach.

Perfecting your imaginative powers is a constant effort that requires limit-free thinking. Giving up control and surrendering to the process of creating a vision requires a keen sense of imagination. Find that child inside of you who once dreamed of being a great dancer, baseball player, or astronaut and spend some time alone with him or her. Let your thoughts be still and try to recapture the joy of an untroubled moment. If you make a habit of taking these "imagination breaks" to think of every possible way you could improve your job, no matter how silly, your mind will become more flexible and open to new ideas. You will be more willing to share and consider the thoughts of others, and you will be able to collaborate with them to shape good ideas into great ones.

KEEP IT SIMPLE

"When your values are clear to you, making decisions becomes easier."

—Roy E. Disney

LEADING AN ORGANIZATION quickly becomes a complicated endeavor. There are so many moving parts, not to mention people, all of which have distinct considerations and personalities. There are market trends, board approvals, and government regulations to manage and oversee.

My goal is to make your life less complicated, not to add to the confusion. I've already talked about how leadership is not one-size-fits-all, but a unique path for every individual. To offer a highly-detailed map for successful leadership would be counter to my own beliefs and counterproductive for your own progress. People often overthink methodologies because they believe that adding more details will guarantee they can get it right. This is one more manifestation of the illusion of control.

You also run the risk of "paralysis by analysis" by overanalyzing the issues at hand, spending too much time gathering data because the direction to act is unclear. In his book *Corps Business*, David Freedman writes about the Marine Corps' 70 percent solution principle. He writes, "By promoting the 70 percent solution, Marines do not advocate shoot-from-the-hip decision-making. Neither do they condone foolish plans. But they do caution against waiting until all the angles are figured out. Instead, when time is of the essence, Marines act as soon as they have a plan with a good chance of working." The idea is to get 70 percent of what you need to know, create a good plan based on that knowledge, and then to get started. You will soon see if you have selected the right course and will be able to adjust or course-correct as needed.

Success for a Visionary Leader is mostly about mindset. The rest of this book will be based upon my own formula for success, which, for the sake of simplicity, is called the Success Formula. While not strictly a mathematical equation, the Success Formula accounts for the three critical stages a Visionary Leader goes through to achieve a vision.

The three phases of the Success Formula are Create, Commit, and Execute. Although the equation is simple, each step requires tremendous dedication and plenty of hard work.

I'll note that the Success Formula assumes you are already a Visionary Leader, a designation which requires a fair amount of preparation. The entire first part of this book has been focused on cultivating the mindset of a Visionary Leader. Revisit these ideas often: one read-through is not enough to absorb everything. Once you have the proper perspective in place, you can move on to the next chapters, which cover each phase of the Success Formula.

PART III

CREATING
THE VISION

Once you have spent some time preparing your mindset as a Visionary Leader, you can start to create your vision. Cultivating your mindset is an ongoing process of growth and evolution, one which you will need to maintain as you move through the different phases of the Success Formula. To create the vision, you first need to ask yourself what you are trying to achieve and why you are trying to achieve it. Clarifying the answers to these two key questions and you will be able to solidify a vision that you can explain, describe, and get other people excited about.

LEARN THE TRUE IMPORTANCE OF VISION

"The right vision is an idea so energizing that it in effect jump-starts the future by calling forth skills, talents, and resources to make it happen."

—Burt Nanus

WE TAKE THE IDEA OF VISION FOR GRANTED in today's society. It's a buzzword that is often used without a full grasp of its meaning.

Having a vision means to see a picture of the future so clearly and completely that it becomes your second reality. The principles of manifestation and the laws of attraction state that the stronger your vision is, the easier it becomes to bring it to fruition. I keep returning to the infinite universe and the infinite six inches of space between your ears, but here they come again: if you can create a vision that lives clearly in the infinite space of your mind, it's no different than a vision that lives clearly in the infinite space of the universe. Everything you see around you right now was created out of thin air. The chair you are sitting in, the house that you live in, the office you work in all started as ideas which human beings turned into reality. Never underestimate the capability of the human mind, and remember, your mind is no different from the mind of any other successful person on this earth.

Do you know a child who knew by the age of seven what she wanted to be when she grew up? This little girl decided exactly what she wanted and didn't waver through elementary, middle, or high school. Her vision was strong through college and after graduation. This young woman is now out there in the world, successfully doing whatever it is she said she would be doing twenty-plus years ago.

Do you know a child who didn't seem to have much ambition or desire to be anything? This little boy was unsure of his major in college, which took extra time to complete. Around age thirty, he was living with his parents, still undecided and unsure of the trajectory of his career and of his life in general.

What's the difference between those two stories? One child had a vision, the other didn't. For the first child, a personal vision kept her on course, and she was continuously taking actions that moved her closer to her goals. For the second child, a lack of vision meant he was never quite sure where he was headed, so he never had a clear sense of what action he ought to take next. All roads lead to the same place if you don't know where you are going.

Visions can change, and the careers we dream of as children may not be the right fit once we mature into adults. For an individual with vision, however, these shifts are made through subtle course corrections. You continuously measure where you are headed against your values, interests, and what makes you happy. Even if you have a change of heart, you have honed and practiced the skills of holding a vision for yourself and learning how to achieve it. The universe is generous to those who generously put themselves into the universe and are willing to go forth and seek what it is they desire.

GIVE YOURSELF
A CLEAR DIRECTION

*"At the center of your being, you have the answer; you
know who you are and you know what you want."*

—Lao Tzu

HOW DO YOU READ A MAP if you don't know where you're headed? What
good is a compass if you're not sure whether you're going north or south?
Without a vision, you are adrift, aimless, and wandering. Some might argue
that being aimless allows for interesting and unexpected experiences. I sub-
mit that you can still have interesting and unexpected experiences, if you

stay open to messages from the universe, while moving toward your goals. Furthermore, not having a sense of where you're going doesn't lead to wandering so much as it leads to paralysis. When you don't know which direction you are headed in, you are afraid to ever take a step. Your goals can shift; your dreams can change, but you've got to start somewhere. Otherwise, you may look around decades later and find that you've never really gone anywhere at all.

CREATE A MISSION STATEMENT USING SMALL WORDS WITH BIG MEANING

"You will derive your best ideas when you strip away non-essentials and stay focused on the basics."

—Stanley M. Davis

ONCE YOU HAVE A VISION, you must find a means to describe it to others, to get it out of your head and into the world. Nobody can see inside your mind except you, but with carefully chosen words you can paint a crystal-clear picture of the future you see unfolding.

It is vital that you describe your vision in words that are simple and clear. This is harder than it looks. Although the message is simple, the meaning behind the message must be carefully considered. You must also understand that as a leader, your words have significant impact, and even the simplest of words have a huge depth of complexity behind them.

Making anything simple requires some thought. The natural human tendency is to explain complex ideas with even greater complexity and content. Rather than clarify our ideas, we make them more difficult to understand. Forming a mission statement requires an in-depth understanding of the history, culture, principles, and aspirations of the organization, but it also demands that this understanding be distilled into clear, digestible language.

There are many layers of thought and discovery required to be able to define the terms of a mission statement clearly and succinctly. My process for creating a mission statement has five steps:

- First, take some time to write a brief history of the organization. Define the organization's purpose, the values of its founders, and the trajectory of its growth over the years. This document should highlight the traditions, points of philosophy, goals, and business approaches of the organization.

- Second, in a few brief words or phrases, define the company's culture. You may wish to maintain the current culture, but if you wish to shift or change the company culture, describe the results of that shift.

- Third, define the unbreakable principles of the organization. These are the organization's most important values which as a Visionary Leader you have a sacred obligation to preserve.

- Fourth, articulate your vision of what the organization aspires to become.

- Finally, use this information to create the organization's mission statement. A mission statement must be short, concise, clear, and enduring. It should reflect the company's deepest values and act as a compass for where the organization is headed. Work with an editor to get the language right.

A mission statement tells the world why you exist and what you stand for. It also serves as a guiding light for employees and will anchor the organization's culture, strategies, policies, and infrastructure for decades to come. Strategies change, but missions do not.

To put this into context, let's look at a few examples. The mission statement of one of my previous organizations was *"to provide superior healthcare and an exceptional patient-centered experience."*

This mission statement is straightforward, easy both to understand and to agree with: Who doesn't want to provide superior healthcare and an exceptional patient-centered experience? However, it's important to realize that these terms were unique to our organization. We used highly specific criteria in four key results areas (patient experience, top decile performance, one standard of care, and financial stability) to determine whether we were achieving our mission. This required a deep understanding of what superior healthcare and an exceptional patient-centered experience meant to us.

Some other examples of excellent mission statements include:

- General Electric: *To invent the next industrial era, to build, move, power and cure the world.*

- The Humane Society: *Celebrating Animals, Confronting Cruelty.*

- The USO: *The USO strengthens America's military service members by keeping them connected to family, home and country, throughout their service to the nation.*

- Mayo Clinic: *To inspire hope, and contribute to health and well-being by providing the best care to every patient through integrated clinical practice, education and research.*

ADD REAL VALUE
WITH YOUR MISSION

"From my very first day as an entrepreneur, I've felt the only mission worth pursuing in business is to make people's lives better."

—Richard Branson

AS A VISIONARY LEADER, what you create must add real value to both your organization and society at large. Creating a vision that does not add significant value may be a fun, imaginative exercise, but it will not give your organization a purposeful mission. I define a "mission" differently than a "goal", in that a goal can be set for any reason. You might set a goal because it's fun, to see if you can, or to determine how life would be if you could. A mission, on the other hand, is never arbitrary.

It is possible to go down a rabbit hole of creativity, adding layer upon layer of innovation, but at the end of the day, that isn't practical for a large organization. This kind of free-form expression and ingenuity has a place and can even add value to society, but it doesn't belong in the realm of Visionary Leadership. One of the responsibilities of a Visionary Leader is to stand at a higher point on the hillside than others. From this vantage point, you can see and hear and discuss things nobody else does. Your worldview is of a broader horizon, but until you get folks up on the hillside with you, they may not be able to see from your perspective.

As a Visionary Leader, your carefully crafted mission is your compass. If you are the head of a large organization, chasing impractical ideas is not a worthy enterprise. The entrepreneurial climate of our culture means that a great many young people have really cool ideas, particularly when it comes to tech-related initiatives. While I support this creativity and innovation on a personal level, when I was the leader of an organization, I knew that many of these ideas were either not feasible or did not add value to my organization's mission. One of the key ways healthcare differs from the tech industry is that healthcare is focused on longevity. The executives of these organizations are working on 100-year visions to make their companies sustainable long-term. The startup culture may appeal to many other industries, but to a healthcare CEO it sounds like a flash in the pan. Striking this balance between innovation and practical realities is an important, ever-evolving task of the Visionary Leader.

ALWAYS ASK, "WHAT'S NEXT?"

"Adapt or perish, now as ever, is nature's inexorable imperative."

—H.G. Wells

THERE'S A COMMON MISCONCEPTION that Visionary Leaders have a mystical ability to see the future. I'd like to dispel that myth here and now. Visionary Leaders aren't mystics. They are pragmatic realists who are open to reinvention and use outside-the-box thinking to anticipate trends and shifts in their organizations and industries.

To do this, the Visionary Leader is constantly looking beyond the horizon and around the corner. Although these two terms seem interchangeable, they have some slight differences. Looking beyond the horizon is heading toward the future, seeing a picture of what's possible and moving an organization toward it. On the other hand, looking around the corner must do with anticipating shifts in the market, the industry, the economy, and the company culture. Many "unexpected changes" in fact give clear signs well in advance to those who are open and willing to consider alternate possibilities.

When you look around the corner, you are trying to access a space where you don't know what you don't know. If you can get a tiny glimmer of in-

sight into that infinite realm of possibility, that's all you need to figure some things out. How far out can you realistically envision the future? What's beyond that? Your guesses are informed by your experience, the speed of change, the organization's capabilities, and other factors within the environment and the economy. If you're asking the right questions, your subconscious mind will be doing a lot of this work for you, filtering through key information to your conscious mind and providing you with answers.

Whether you are staring off beyond the sun or trying to peek down the avenue, the goal is to make a prediction about what will happen next and to shift directions without straying too far from the organization's current growth and objectives. A Visionary Leader must understand the difference between a course correction and a U-turn. If an organization's mission has been thoughtfully articulated and its leadership is continually looking ahead, U-turns should be far and few between.

How do you get into this forward-thinking mindset? First, acknowledge that there will be a lot of risk and a good deal of guesswork involved. Anticipating the future involves a combination of factors, including trying to understand everything around you, reading about what other experts are forecasting, looking backward at where growth areas have been in the past, and charting the trajectory of where they seem to be heading in the present. All this data informs your thinking as you ask the question, "What's next?"

Of course, once you've identified what the future might hold, it's equally important that you take action to move your organization in the right direction. Stick with me for a moment while I tell you about one of my favorite animals: the duck-billed platypus.

Neither the strongest of creatures nor the smartest, the duck-billed platypus has somehow managed to meet the criteria for "survival of the fittest". The platypus' secret to survival has been its ability to adapt and change to its surrounding environment. Hence, we get this charming little animal, an odd combination of mammal and bird, which has somehow withstood the challenges of time.

When Charles Darwin wrote about evolution and natural selection, I'm sure he had no idea that his research would be so applicable to the business world of the twenty-first century.

As a Visionary Leader, you must evolve and adapt to your surroundings. The changes you make may not be elegant or graceful, but having a duck-billed platypus of an organization is certainly better than having no organization at all. You must be willing to acknowledge and face the obstacles and challenges that appear before you and be prepared to do what's difficult in order for the company to survive. Sticking with the status quo is never really a successful option if you want to survive.

SEE NEGATIVE SPACES AND POLARITY

"I know it like the back of my hand."

—English Idiom

HERE'S A QUESTION: how well do you actually know the back of your hand? Take a few minutes to examine it, and while you're at it, take a look at the palm as well. Notice the way one side corresponds to the other: the ridges of the knuckles on one side correlate to the folds in the fingers on the palm. There's polarity between the two sides.

Now think about an x-ray image, the way the light and dark work together to create one single picture. The negative space is just as important as the positive space. Without one, the other would be meaningless.

American Indians of the Apache tribe in the southwest used to evade the U.S. Cavalry using the principle of negative space. They would hide in the places between the cacti, in plain sight, but in areas where the human eye was unaccustomed to focusing. We tend to focus on objects themselves, rather than the spaces between them.

Look at the image below. You've probably seen something like this before, with the caption "Is it a vase or two faces?" The answer, of course, is that it's both. It just depends on how your mind classifies positive and negative space.

Your mind tends to easily identify either the vase or the two faces; it takes more concentration to see the second image. Visionary Leaders possess the ability to look beyond their natural inclinations and see the possibilities that aren't readily apparent.

It's a challenging task to be smarter than your own human tendencies. Visionary Leaders need to be able to take a problem and spend time thinking about it as a polarity, to understand how the palm of the hand relates to the back of the hand, to recognize that a change to one side will automatically create a shift in the other.

Recognize that objects are equally as important as the spaces between them. Learn to see what's in plain sight that most people overlook. Consider various angles of a situation. Understanding other perspectives not only gives insight into how to affect change, it allows you to more thoroughly anticipate the repercussions of your choices.

UNDERSTAND THE THREE KINDS OF KNOWLEDGE

"There are known knowns. These are things we know that we know. There are known unknowns. There are things that we know we don't know. But there are also unknown unknowns. There are things we don't know we don't know."

—Donald Rumsfeld

HERE'S HOW TO UNDERSTAND the three kinds of knowledge and how they relate to one another in scope.

Take a dime to represent the first kind of knowledge. This is "Everything that you know that you know". You know how to tie a pair of shoes, to throw a football, to play the piano.

Now, take a cup to represent the second kind of knowledge. This is "Everything that you know that you don't know". You don't really know how a computer functions, or how photosynthesis works, or how to speak ancient Greek (unless you're an engineer, a biologist, and a linguist). Drop the dime into the cup for some perspective.

Next, take the building you are in to represent the third kind of knowledge. This is "Everything that you don't know that you don't know". The building is only a representation, as the third kind of knowledge is bigger

93

than anything you can imagine. This stands for all the ideas you've never heard of in the books you've never read, all the pieces of art you've never seen, and all the scientific principles that remain undiscovered. It represents every good idea that hasn't yet been thought of or contemplated. It is the continually expanding universe.

Even as the first two kinds of knowledge increase, as your own processing and understanding expands, the third kind of knowledge constantly outpaces you, a skyscraper looming over a tiny dime.

Rather than fear the infinite scope of knowledge, embrace it. Getting curious about the things you don't know will help you develop a bigger capacity for opening your mind to capture new thoughts and ideas. Honing skills such as meditation will help you recognize and access the unbelievable power you didn't previously know that you possessed. The universe is infinite, but so are you. Think about the moment when man discovered fire and what a revolution that was. Then, think about where we were 100 years ago and the rapid advancements that have brought us to where we are today. Just imagine the progress we might make in the next 100 years. Knowing that there is information that you don't know that you don't know can be terrifying—or incredibly exciting. Which will you choose?

Stay open
to new messages
and messengers

*"If you do not expect the unexpected you will not find
it, for it is not to be reached by search or trail."*

—Heraclitus

WHEN YOU RELEASE YOURSELF FROM THE ILLUSION OF CONTROL, you gain access to all the messages the universe is sending about opportunities for change and growth. Messages are simply new information or possibilities that come your way. You receive thousands of messages every day, more than your conscious mind can possibly process. So, your subconscious mind uses your belief structures to automatically filter and interpret these messages, to create the life you believe you have been "given".

These messages are interconnected with all the threads of your life. I make it a point to always explore new opportunities, especially if they show up out of the blue. If a friend tells me "You ought to go to lunch with this guy," there's a message in that. I'm not committing to anything, I'm just having lunch. This type of exploration may reveal key insights into the part of the universe that makes up what you don't know you don't know. Messages can help fit pieces of the puzzle of your life together in unexpected, but fascinating and often deeply fulfilling ways.

You've probably had the experience of being in the shower or driving to work when suddenly a solution or innovation pops into your head. Where did that thought come from? From somewhere "out there". You can say it came from God, or the cosmos, or another dimension. The expanding universe and the six inches of space between your ears are essentially one and the same.

How do you get to a place where you can let your mind run free to explore different possibilities? By looking around the corner and beyond the horizon. By examining polarities and negative spaces. These techniques will help you stimulate your mind in a different way and open your senses.

Remember that your brain needs clear priorities about what's important to send you the most helpful information possible. You give your subconscious specific instructions by getting into a quiet place, stilling your mind, and asking yourself the questions you need answered.

Your subconscious mind is why you get your best ideas in the shower or on your commute. As you begin to align your conscious and subconscious mind around your vision and stop trying to control every effort consciously, you will see more effectively the connections between the messages that you are receiving and the value that they have in helping you reach your vison.

Talk to yourself (and thereby your subconscious) every day about the vision you want to accomplish. Your subconscious mind will pick up on that vision and mark it "important" among all the thousands of pieces of information you take in every moment. You become what you think about, and what better way to integrate and embody your vision than by truly becoming it? Think about what you need, ask yourself the right questions, then forget it all and watch as the answers start coming to you. This is a continuous process that keeps feeding and refining your vision.

Here's a humorous example of a message that came out of nowhere, in the middle of the night.

When I was in my administrative residency at the University of Kansas Medical Center, I lived in a tiny little apartment. I had just moved in, so I didn't have a phone yet, but I did have a beeper because I was working as part of the hospital administration. In case you're too young to remember, when you get paged on your beeper, you need a phone so you can call the number back and find out what the person wants. When my beeper would go off, I would get up, get dressed, climb into my red Volkswagen Beetle, and drive to the 7-Eleven, which had a payphone on the wall outside the building, to return the page.

Well, I got beeped at 2 A.M. one night. It was right in the middle of a massive thunderstorm, practically raining sideways. I stood there at the payphone with my raincoat on, getting absolutely soaked. I dialed the number on the pager and told them I was the administrator on call.

The voice on the other end said she just wanted me to know that there was a severe thunderstorm warning in the area.

No kidding.

I thanked her for the update and said, "Please don't beep me when the all clear is announced."

What was the point of this message? I honestly don't know, besides giving me a good story and a deep appreciation for cell phones. However, I do believe that there will be messages that arrive in the middle of the night. As a leader, you must be prepared for anything and willing to answer the call—literally.

Not only is a Visionary Leader always receiving messages, he or she should be a messenger as well. One way I deliver messages is by dropping ideas at people's feet (this is what happened when I introduced my daughter to *Unlimited Power*). Throughout my entire career, I dropped ideas at people's feet just to see what they would do with them. I was always delighted when an individual's unique talents and creativity turned one of those ideas into a marvelous success, far exceeding my expectations for what the idea could become.

The people who picked up my ideas and ran with them have become some of my favorite leadership success stories. As a Visionary Leader, you might make a request of someone to see what he or she is capable of or whether he or she is willing to seize an opportunity and run with it.

In Napoleon Hill's book, *Think and Grow Rich*, he tells the story of a man who had a farm in Africa and wanted to become wealthy. The man left his farm and traveled the world seeking fame and fortune. After many trials and failures, he returned to his farm in Africa, broke and dejected. One day, he saw something sparkle in the creek bed nearby and discovered acres of diamonds lying just below the surface. The answer we are looking for has often been right in front of us all along. The key is whether we are prepared enough to know where to look.

Sometimes, the messages you're receiving encourage you not to take action. Have you ever been faced with a problem, done nothing, and found that eventually, the solution appeared? Sometimes, "wait and see" is the best approach you can possibly take. This is different from burying your head in the sand and ignoring the problem. The choice to "wait and see" must be a conscious one, not a default that comes about because the Visionary Leader is too afraid to act. If you wait for the sky to open and tell you what to do next, you'll be waiting an awfully long time.

To be honest, sometimes wait and see feels like a wise and prescient decision, and sometimes it just feels like you got lucky and things worked out. Yet, the concept does speak to the idea that while visionaries need to be bold, they should never be reckless. When you're making decisions that affect an entire organization, you don't want to act before you have all the relevant information, including a sense of the way your choices will impact every single member of the company. If the unknowns are too significant, staying in the same place temporarily may end up being an excellent way of moving forward.

An effective Visionary Leader must be willing to take risks—when the timing is right. There will be times when you buck the status quo and lead your organization into uncharted territory. Every major decision you make must have a strategic upside associated with it. The directional changes you make should follow the Success Formula, starting with a vision of where the organization is going, securing the commitment of everyone involved, and possessing the willingness to do whatever it takes to get there.

In the course of my career, I have failed and been disappointed many times. Most of the failures were the result of trying to implement strategies where other organizations were involved. In the merger and acquisition world, there are many opportunities that look and feel right, but fail because both sides are unwilling to enter a true partnership.

When the risk of failure is high, my best advice is always to start with shared culture, principles, and strategies. Clearly define what both parties need to have to make the deal and what they are willing to leave behind. Do not deceive yourself that you can change a major deal point down the road and do not feel like there is any critical timeline that must be followed. Going slowly or walking away are often valuable tactics that may make a deal more favorable at a future date down the road.

Another key factor is anticipating all the possibilities if you take a risk and it doesn't work out. What will your fallback position be? How much of a financial, political, or emotional impact will the errant step have on the organization, the assets, the people you are responsible for, and your own career? If the liabilities are too great, then consider a different strategy or a staged strategy to get to your goal. When an industry goes through a major correction, like the banking and airline industries have, the imminent threat of ultimate failure may force you to take a major risk. This is where your Visionary Leadership skills will be most important.

USE MEDITATION
AS A VISIONING TOOL

*"How we feel about ourselves, the joy we get from living,
ultimately depend directly on how the mind filters and
interprets everyday experiences. Whether we are happy
depends on inner harmony, not on the controls we are
able to exert over the great forces of the universe."*

—Mihaly Csikszentmihalyi

THE PRACTICE OF MEDITATION IS THOUSANDS OF YEARS OLD, and science now strongly supports what wisdom traditions have known for years: it's an extremely beneficial practice for both body and mind. People use meditation to lower their blood pressure, reduce anxiety, and increase happiness. Meditation has been linked to better health in a plethora of different ways.

For the Visionary Leader, meditation can bring you a stilled, quiet head space. When your mind is calm, there are two things that happen:

First, you can focus on creating your vision. You want your vision to be so solid you can walk around in it and survey the landscape. Get a feel for the smells, textures, noises, and colors of the world you're creating. Embed in your brain what you want to accomplish and continually reinforce it by visiting that space often. When you meditate, your mind can let go of other things and concentrate on fleshing out your vision until it becomes tangible to you.

Second, meditation gives you more room for innovation. Not only are you able to ask your subconscious the questions you need answered in a more articulate way when you're in this state, you're also more receptive to the answers. The ideas are better, more creative, and more free-flowing when you meditate regularly.

Meditation describes a state when time stands still, your mind is clear, your body feels no pain, and you exist in a complete sense of presence. Most of us have had at least one moment where we experienced this state, which Mihaly Csikszentmihalyi calls "flow", and most of us also long to experience it again. This heightened experience is available to all of us, not just a few talented athletes, poets, or songwriters. To achieve it, you must change your perspective of time and its relationship to experience. Meditation is a tool to shift that perspective.

Most Eastern and Western philosophies and religions offer up their own meditative practices. You can meditate while siting, lying, walking, or standing. Mantras, chants, and breathing techniques may be part of the process. I am not an expert in meditation by any means, but I have included several recommendations in the Reading List that give you examples of techniques that I have studied. The following is an excerpt from the writing of Giovanni Dienstmann, founder of *Live and Dare* (liveanddare.com), who describes the following three categories of meditation techniques:

> ### FOCUSED ATTENTION MEDITATION
> *Focusing the attention on a single object during the whole meditation session. This object may be the breath, a mantra, visualization, part of the body, external object, etc. As the practitioner advances, his ability to keep the flow of attention in the chosen object gets stronger, and distractions become less common and short-lived. Both the depth and*

steadiness of his attention are developed. Examples of these are: Samatha (Buddhist meditation), some forms of Zazen, Loving Kindness Meditation, Chakra Meditation, Kundalini Meditation, Sound Meditation, Mantra Meditation, Pranayama, some forms of Qigong, and many others.

OPEN MONITORING MEDITATION

Instead of focusing the attention on any one object, we keep it open, monitoring all aspects of our experience, without judgment or attachment. All perceptions, be them [sic] internal (thoughts, feelings, memory, etc.) or external (sound, smell, etc.), are recognized and seen for what they are. It is the process of non-reactive monitoring of the content of experience from moment to moment, without going into them. Examples are: Mindfulness meditation (vipassana), as well as some types of Taoist meditation.

EFFORTLESS PRESENCE

It's the state where the attention is not focused on anything in particular, but reposes on itself—quiet, empty, steady, and introverted. We can also call it "Choiceless Awareness" or "Pure Being". Most of the meditation quotes you find speak of this state.

This is the true purpose behind all kinds of meditation, and not a meditation type in itself. All traditional techniques of meditation recognize that the object of focus, and even the process of monitoring, is just a means to train the mind, so that effortless inner silence and deeper states of consciousness can be discovered. Eventually, both the object of focus and the process itself is [sic] left behind, and there is only left the true self of the practitioner, as "pure presence".

—◀○▶—

My own personal meditation practice most closely resembles the Effortless Presence technique. I sit in a comfortable arm chair in a comfortable room and ensure that I have thirty to forty-five minutes of uninterrupted time available. I close my eyes and begin to relax by concentrating on my breathing. I breathe slowly and rhythmically: four seconds to inhale, two to three seconds between breaths, and four seconds to exhale. I focus on my nostrils where the breath is coming in and going out and keep relaxing.

As a reformed Type A personality, being patient and thought-less was very difficult for me at first. As I meditated more often, I could increase the amount of time that I could go without thinking. The most important skills you can cultivate in meditation are patience and self-compassion.

Remember that you're not forcing anything in meditation; in fact, to work effectively, you need to get your mind to the place where you're completely relaxed. Meditation is not about thinking; it's about quieting the conscious mind. Trust that your subconscious mind is still hard at work for you, gathering and filtering the information it needs from the world around you to make the answers to your questions clear.

When you find yourself thinking about something, simply go back to the thing you are focusing on and clear your thoughts again. Some people hold an image in their mind, like a white bird or a spinning top. Over time you will find long periods of thought-lessness and quiet. After meditation, you will experience a sense of relaxation and clear-headed thinking that you may never have experienced before. You may find that during periods of meditation, or shortly after you stop, your mind will suddenly receive an idea or an answer to a problem that has been a priority for you. When this occurs, you will truly understand the value of meditation for the Visionary Leader.

STUDY
OUTSIDE YOUR FIELD

"Breakthrough ideas are most often 'intersectional' and occur when we bring concepts from one field into a new, unfamiliar territory."

—Frans Johansson

THE ERA OF THE RENAISSANCE saw a huge expansion of knowledge in the world. During this period, dozens of creative geniuses pushed and inspired one another to dizzying heights of greatness in art, science, and technology. According to Frans Johansson, author of *The Medici Effect*, it was the unique interdisciplinary collaborations of this time that made the Renaissance such an extraordinary time of breakthroughs and achievements.

Johansson's book is named after the Medici, a wealthy Italian family who became great patrons of art and science. During the Renaissance, members of the aristocracy across Europe started to focus on solving challenging problems. They brought together the greatest minds from different fields and used their collective expertise to work out creative, innovative solutions. Bringing in people from different fields of knowledge brought different perspectives that hadn't previously been considered, shaping and shifting new ways of thinking.

The same principles that made the Renaissance so great still hold true today. If you want to be a pioneer in your own industry, you should look outside your field for fresh insight and inspiration. Of course, there's an infinite amount of information outside your field of study available out there, so how do you know where to begin? I like to start with a challenge my organization is facing and then look to see how other industries would tackle a similar problem.

One such challenge was dealing with the changes that came from the passage of the Affordable Care Act, namely, maintaining high quality standards for healthcare while keeping costs down. Our organization needed an innovative way to make those two things work together instead of in opposition. The question I formulated around this problem was "What is the key interaction in our organization that will have the biggest impact on our health system?"

I knew this key interaction would be something that was repeated over and over again inside the company. It was really this question that got me thinking about particles, those simple elements which together build up huge layers of complexity. This is when I started considering quantum physics, to see what insights I could glean. From there, I learned how the universe is always seeking balance, and that even in the face of chaotic events on a grand scale, those tiny particles are still somehow perfectly aligned.

When I returned to the issue within my organization, I could see that the key interaction we needed to address was the moment when a doctor decided to write an order for a patient. While our physicians had always made good clinical decisions, they now needed to make good value-based decisions as well. Once I understood this interaction, the next steps were clear. We needed to provide physicians with the education to help them make decisions that were both clinically and financially sound.

Looking outside my field of study helped me find a new solution for my industry-specific problem. I suggest starting this kind of investigation with a question related to your organization. From there, let your mind wander to identify other approaches that will help you find creative, original solutions.

SEEK
OUTSIDE OPINIONS

"A mentor is someone who sees more talent and ability within you than you see in yourself, and helps bring it out of you."

—Bob Proctor

IF YOU WANT TO DEVELOP YOUR FULL POTENTIAL as a Visionary Leader, it is vital that you rely on trusted mentors, peers, and thought leaders to refine your ideas, work through problems, and help you grow. This section is divided into the two main sources for seeking outside opinions in the professional world. Depending on your situation, your family and friends may be beneficial advisors too.

MENTORSHIP:
For the purposes of this book, let's define a mentorship as a relationship in which there is one senior party and one junior party. The senior party is the mentor and the junior party is the mentee. While the most common mentorship arrangement will be a literal expression of the senior/junior relationship, in which the senior person is older than the junior one, that may not always be the case. What distinguishes the senior party as a mentor is experience and a certain depth of wisdom and knowledge that he or she is willing to pass on.

When I was in graduate school, one of my degree requirements was to commit to one of three ways of giving value back to the field: teaching, publishing, or mentoring. My university had a strong alumni program that offered significant mentorship opportunities, and the idea of giving value back through mentorship has stuck with me. Mentoring is an important part of the acculturalization of people entering the work force. The apprenticeships that were pervasive in previous centuries are long gone, but at its core, leadership is no different than learning a trade. Mentorships are a way of passing knowledge on from leader to leader.

I highly advise all leaders, regardless of age or job title, to find at least one mentor during their careers. You should look for somebody who understands how you are trying to shape your career and who will give you honest feedback.

Where do mentors come from? To some extent, an individual's boss always provides some level of guidance and mentorship. In arrangements such as leadership development programs, the manager may offer structured coaching and skill-building to help the employee reach his or her goals.

Of course, Visionary Leaders tend to be at the top of the food chain in their organizations, so while looking to one's manager may be valuable on the way up, it doesn't make much sense once you become the CEO. To find mentors, I suggest thinking about who you respect and admire. The easiest place to start is by considering the people you already know. These people do not have to hold your same job title or even be in your industry. They do need to hold similar values to you and be examples of what you would like to emulate in your own career.

Mentorship may begin as a more formal relationship with regular meeting dates or it may start with a simple request to meet for coffee and ask for some advice. Some mentors will impart their wisdom by challenging you. Years later, I can look back and recognize various individuals I worked with and for as mentors. Paid coaches may also act as mentors in certain situations.

It takes real courage to lead an organization in a different direction. Developing the required skills come from experience, but also through observation. A strong relationship with an excellent mentor can teach you valuable lessons, but keep in mind that even a terrible manager provides a learning opportunity by being an example of what a leader should not do. Learning from others is critical to your continued success.

MASTERMINDS:

A mastermind differs from a mentorship in a couple of key ways: first, masterminds are structured in a group format, where mentorships are usually one-to-one, and second, masterminds are composed of peers sharing ideas with one another, rather than a senior individual advising a junior individual. The idea of masterminds comes from Napoleon Hill's *Think and Grow Rich*, which I discuss more in the next section.

Try to be part of at least one mastermind group, particularly one composed of people in different industries. By joining one of these groups, you have the chance to learn from the lessons and mistakes of others. If you actively participate, presenting your ideas and soliciting feedback, you will get ingenuous solutions and perspectives on the challenges facing your organization. Masterminds are a great place to iron out the kinks in your ideas and to test your theories in a safe space. You want to ensure that any proposals you bring to your organization have been thoroughly vetted before you take them to your team. Before joining a mastermind, you need to have cultivated the Visionary Leader's mindset, especially a healthy sense of self-esteem, so you can receive feedback as openly as possible.

One particular mastermind experience stands out to me: for many years, I was in a group of colleagues who would call up one another to discuss specific problems within their organizations. These folks were not all healthcare executives; they were lawyers, doctors, entrepreneurs, educators, and more. One member of this group worked in large industries, anticipating and implementing directional changes and industry-wide shifts. In 2010, healthcare was facing a huge directional change, and so I called up Herman and asked for his help.

Herman always wanted me to boil down the problem into a fundamental question. Then, we'd spend half a day coming up with related topics and potential answers. For this session, the question I came up with was: how do we shift gears as a healthcare organization from fee-for-service to a value-based model?

Herman considered my question for a moment, then wrote a single word on the white board: ecosystem.

We were off and running. His viewpoint helped me frame healthcare as an ecosystem and that changed the way we thought about the shift and the impact it would have on every aspect of the industry. Herman shared some of the research he had done for a project with the BBC, and although entertainment doesn't seem closely related to healthcare, his conclusions brought a much-needed fresh perspective to the problem. This session was critical in developing the volume-to-value approach that ultimately addresses the needs of the healthcare industry and anticipates the ways in which it continues to evolve.

READ BIOGRAPHIES

"Learn as if you were going to live forever."

—Larry and Hersch Wilson

WHEN I WAS IN GRADUATE SCHOOL, we had a series of guest lecturers come into one of my classes. Every Wednesday at noon, we'd bring brown bag lunches and listen to a speaker talk about relevant topics in the healthcare field. One such lecture has stuck with me—in part because it took me so long to grasp the speaker's lesson.

The lecture was by an eminent hospital executive, and all the students were excited about the opportunity to learn from this august leader. We were attentively waiting when he entered the room, and among each other, we later discussed just how comfortable we had felt in his presence. He greeted us warmly and asked us questions about our lives. He shared quips and stories about his years at the university. While we enjoyed making small talk with him, we were wondering when he was going to start the lecture and let us in on the secrets of the profession.

We knew the moment had come when he looked at us and said, "I have one piece of advice for you." With baited breath, we waited for him to set forth the pearl of wisdom that would ensure our success.

To our surprise, he simply said, "Read biographies."

Then, he went on to talk about his boat, his grandchildren, and his vacation plans for next summer. When he finished and walked out of the room we looked at each other in disbelief. What did he mean by read biographies? How could that advice help launch our careers?

Years later, I discovered this man was wiser than I had ever imagined. He knew that some of us would remember what he had laid at our feet and that his cryptic advice would return to us repeatedly. He also knew that some of us would have to actually take his advice to discover for ourselves the lesson he had succinctly distilled into just two words.

I have read dozens of biographies in the last few decades. A few of my favorites appear below and in the Reading List at the end of this book. By spending a good deal of time with these books, all accounts of real people who have made their way through this world, I finally understand what he was getting at. The lesson I believe he wished to impart is that to be successful, we must first discover that we are each unique, different from everybody else, but no better or worse. By reading biographies, we uncover the pure humanity of great people: their successes and failures, their self-doubts and human foibles. We understand that they too are unique, but no better or worse than anybody else—including us.

Selected Biographies

Lincoln by David Herbert Donald

$E=mc^2$: *A biography of the World's Most Famous Equation* by David Bodanis

Einstein: His Life and Universe by Walter Isaacson

Reminiscences by Douglas MacArthur (Autobiography)

Richard M. Nixon: A Life in Full by Conrad Black

The Wizard of Menlo Park: How Thomas Alva Edison Invented the Modern world by Randall E. Stross

Thomas Jefferson: Author of America by Cristopher Hitchens

The Seven Storey Mountain: An Autobiography of Faith by Thomas Merton

Wilson by A. Scott Berg

The Last Lion: Winston Spencer Churchill: Defender of the Realm, 1940-1965 by William Manchester & Paul Reid

PART IV

COMMITTING TO THE VISION

IN THE FIRST PHASE OF THE SUCCESS FORMULA, you learned how to create your vision. In the second phase, you'll learn how to commit yourself and others to the vision you have created. This is where you get your entire team to see your picture of the future. Commitment is about each employee taking personal ownership and illustrating a complete willingness to support the vision for the organization and the individual who leads it—you.

The cornerstone of commitment is trust. Individuals in your organization won't commit to something they don't believe in, and they won't believe in an idea if they don't inherently trust the person putting the idea forward. While your team must be able to clearly articulate and endorse your vision, they don't need to understand every detail of its implementation, so long as they have faith in the person running the show.

As a Visionary Leader, your role in this second phase of the Success Formula is to interpret your vision back to the people who will ultimately bring that vision to life. Innovation always requires pushing against the status quo, and you may encounter resistance to strategies that are new, different, and unfamiliar. You need to simultaneously have a crystal-clear vision of what you want to create and be flexible enough to let the vision shift based on the feedback you receive. As you seek to communicate your vision in simple terms, allow the vision to evolve and be refined. Boldly ask questions of others. Is this the right path? Are there other options I haven't considered? What would I improve? Listen thoughtfully and thoroughly to their responses.

As CEO, there are very few great organizational reforms I can take credit for. For the most part, all I did was provide a vision, earn people's trust, and allow them to do the work required to achieve the vision in their own way. Mutual trust built mutual confidence, which helped my employees do and be their best. I provided access to the right resources, but it was our skilled and talented team that really made things happen.

Committing to the Vision is by far the most vulnerable phase of the Success Formula for a Visionary Leader. You are offering your ideas to the world, which is a fundamentally uncertain act. There are not guarantees about how your vision will be received. This is why it is so vital that you do the necessary work to create a strong, confident mindset. Ask yourself whether anybody is helping you complete your vision. If the answer is no, why not? What are you avoiding? You may want to revisit the "Preparing for the Journey" section of this book so you can boldly enter this next phase of realizing your vision.

GET PEOPLE TO CARE

"A leader is a person you will follow to a place you wouldn't go by yourself."

—Joel A. Barker

HOW DO YOU GET PEOPLE TO CARE? This is one of the fundamental questions of leadership. You can have the greatest idea in the world, but it won't mean anything if you can't get anybody to care about it. Getting people to care about your vision requires inspiring them. Inspiration stems from high-quality relationships. When you make it clear that you trust and have confidence in your employees, they reciprocate by investing trust and confidence in you. It is characteristically human to rise to the expectations of others. If you believe your team can execute your vision of the future, you will find them remarkably adept at doing so. To inspire, the Visionary Leader must exemplify the highest level of commitment to and confidence in the vision's success.

A Visionary Leader also gets people to care by being prepared. You should be able to describe in detail where your organization is going and do so for anyone who is interested and willing to listen. Do the work required to distill your vision into a clear mission statement.

Invite feedback and input at all levels of your organization. Once your team becomes personally involved, they will be much more connected to the outcome. Recognize that each team member will interpret the vision through his or her own lens and thought process. This is critical to them adopting the vision as their own. However, to ensure that these individual interpretations still adhere closely to the primary vision, it is important to simplify your language. Repeat your message over and over again until you are sure your team clearly understands the message.

I love *The Adventures of Tom Sawyer*, and one of my favorite parts is when Tom Sawyer is painting the fence. By cleverly crafting his "pitch", he enrolls all the neighborhood boys to help him quickly complete the job. Tom's ability to turn an unpleasant chore into a fun and interesting opportunity for others illustrates what can be accomplished when we get people to care.

As a Visionary Leader, you must not only inspire employees with your vision, you must help them identify that vision as their own. I think of this as letting your team put their fingerprints on the vision.

Suppose you broke your employees up into teams and asked them to create an object that allowed you to transport heavy goods from place to place. Without specifically saying so, you described a wheel, and asked each team to "reinvent" it.

The results would be fascinating. Every team would make a wheel that looks and functions a little bit differently. You would have round wheels, oval wheels, wheels made from sticks, stone, and metal. You'd probably even get a square wheel from the team that's always just a little off-the-wall.

When all is said and done, all the teams would have at least one thing in common. Every single team will make their wheel roll. The wheels may not be elegant or efficient, but they will get the job done. Why? Because every team member has participated in the creation of their own wheel. And once it becomes *their* wheel, they will go to any lengths necessary to make sure that wheel does what it's supposed to.

This is the secret behind successful visioning. Once you have created your vision, you must lay it out in such a way that other people understand it. Inspire them by painting a picture of the future and helping them see what's possible. If your vision becomes your employees' vision too, you will be shocked at the effort they will put forth to make that vision a reality. By giving each team responsibility for the vision's success, you allow them to take ownership of the vision itself. Never underestimate the power of ownership.

This requires true belief not only in your vision, but also in the individuals who will be helping you execute it. A Visionary Leader must learn to accept and even embrace wheels of all shapes and sizes.

A Visionary Leader doesn't take resistance to change too personally. State your position, believe in it wholeheartedly, defend it fiercely, but be able to understand the opposite position as well. Your aim is not to like and be liked by everyone on your team, but to operate optimally, you do need mutual respect. Be discerning when selecting your closest circle of advisors. For various reasons, some individuals may be unable to commit to your vision, and all the inspiration, passion, and persuasion in the world will not change their minds. Keep these people out of your inner circle to significantly reduce friction and resistance as you move your organization toward the vision.

Sometimes, it is hard to determine the level of commitment that one of your leaders has to the organization's vision. Passive aggressive behavior is difficult to recognize at first, but becomes evident over time. When it does, you must take swift action.

I once worked with an executive who paid a lot of lip service to our vision. His actions, however, consistently undermined me at every opportunity. Placing one individual above the organization is a luxury the Visionary Leader cannot afford. It wasn't that I took his actions personally. The problem was this executive was detrimental to moving the organization forward. The vision must come first, even if that leads to uncomfortable conversations or letting people go.

Cutting somebody loose is not a fifteen-minute decision; it's a choice made after observation over a period. You need to be patient with people when asking them to make a fundamental shift in the way they do their jobs. Encountering long-term resistance from one or two employees may be an indication that those individuals need to move on. On the other hand, widespread resistance from your team indicates that your vision needs strengthening. There's a big difference between someone being unable to commit to your vision because he or she doesn't understand it and being unable to commit because he or she is not willing to buy in. Use resistance as an opportunity to clarify your argument, refine your message, and to listen to the concerns being voiced. Your position will be stronger for it.

IDENTIFY
THE CRITICAL MOMENT

"You don't need to find a big idea; you can find a little idea that can be made big. Think of something fractional, smaller, simpler, or more focused—all with underlying growth potential."

—Jeremy Gutsche

IN AN EARLIER CHAPTER, I talked about the decision a physician makes when deciding what orders to write for a patient as highly significant for anticipating shifts in the healthcare industry. I think of these kinds of decisions as "critical moments". Critical moments are simple but important interactions, repeated over and over again in an organization, which greatly influence the company's success or failure.

Just how important is the critical moment? Let's take the example above. Healthcare's current business model is built on volume-based transactions. In other words, health systems make money based on the number of procedures they can bill for. This is an unsustainable business model and has been for quite some time. The solution is for healthcare to move to a value-based payment model instead. In a value-based model, the health system would no longer receive payments based on how many procedures it performs. Instead, providers would receive a lump sum of money to keep an individual or family healthy. By necessity, the focus of the industry will be on preventive care and cutting excess in the system, while still performing at high quality standards with excellent outcomes.

The critical moment in this scenario is the decision a physician makes after evaluating a patient. This is because the physician is responsible for determining what tests or procedures are necessary for the patients. Right now, most doctors do not focus on the cost of procedures when making this determination, and there are many cases where doctors order additional testing to cover themselves for liability purposes. If, on the other hand, the physician has the right education, he or she will be able to make a decision that is clinically sound and as cost-effective as possible under the circumstances. For the value-based model to be successful, the physician's mindset around procedure, prescription, and testing must shift 180 degrees.

When you identify the critical moment in a situation, you've pared it down to the smallest unit of change possible. You're working on the subatomic level. Once you've identified the critical moment and the key players involved, you know where your work needs to begin.

USE COLORFUL LANGUAGE TO CONVEY IDEAS

"Inventors are fueled by the analogies that they spot all around them."

—Evan Schwartz

As a leader, my language tends toward vivid images and examples. "Get a firm grip on Jell-O", "Do watch repair with heavy gloves", and "Turn your landing light on", are the kinds of similes, metaphors, and analogies I use when I speak to other leaders and my employees.

Part of this strategy is unintentional: I've always gravitated toward these kinds of phrases. I instinctively recognize that they help clarify ideas for people. Although I have no way to prove it, I have always believed that what got me into graduate school wasn't my grades, but my high score on the Miller Analogies Test (MAT).

As a Visionary Leader, you can consciously employ this kind of language to make a stronger impression on your employees. It's not about trying to impress people; it's about helping them understand you. That's how you get people on board with your way of looking at the world, working hard to make your vision reality.

As a CEO, I used to attend every single orientation for new employees. I showed images of the U.S. Olympic Team and talked about how they were world-class athletes. Every athlete had to work hard and faced major competition for the chance to represent the United States. Then, I'd talk about our organization being world-class. I'd tell new employees that we received 18,000-30,000 job applications per month, and that they had been chosen because they were world-class team members too. They lived up to the expectation, and on the job, their professionalism and commitment truly were world-class.

The language of simile, metaphor, and analogy is most effective when it is basic and understandable to everyone. You need to be able to reach hundreds or thousands of people with different backgrounds and varying degrees of education. Your target audience isn't other executives; it's your average employee. Communicate in clear, accessible language to the people who are working on your vision every day. This not only conveys your ideas effectively, it confirms to your employees that you care about them and the contributions they make.

Make course corrections

"People who cannot invent and reinvent themselves must be content with borrowed postures, secondhand ideas, fitting in instead of standing out."

—Warren Bennis

GROWING UP I WAS ALWAYS INTERESTED IN AIRPLANES. When I was a child, my dad sold all but two acres of our family farm to a dentist. The dentist built an airstrip behind his house, and I loved going down there and watching him take off. The fascination with flying never left me, and I trained and received my pilot's license in 1982.

Flying is a great self-confidence builder and requires increased navigational skills. When you fly, you are very rarely on target. In fact, you spend almost the entire journey slightly off-course. The wind, gravity, and engine dynamics are constantly shifting the plane, so the course must continuously be adjusted for you to arrive at your destination. As the pilot, you first correct in one direction, then the other, and so on for the whole flight.

Visionary Leadership requires course correction too. While you do need a clear destination to make your flight plan, you can never fully predict the trajectory that will take you there. Having the flexibility to course-correct in midair is a valuable skill. You can't anticipate every storm. Unexpected turbulence may suddenly blow you off course. What matters is your ability to recover and refocus on where you're headed.

—◀○▶—

Sooner or later in your career, there will come a time when your strategic path becomes unsustainable due to changes in the environment. It's vital to not only recognize the changes that must occur, but to course-correct as seamlessly as possible.

One such course correction in my own career again concerns those physicians and the volume-to-value shift of the healthcare industry. You'll recall that our organization had determined the single factor with the biggest impact on quality and cost of care was the decision a physician makes at the time of diagnosis. We needed physicians to make judgments that considered both quality and cost of care. The challenge was that we had over 400 physicians on staff with a wide range of backgrounds and training. They were independent thinkers, which made it difficult for us to unify them around one set of best diagnostic practices.

To make the necessary course correction, we first proposed that all our doctors go through training to learn about the changes that needed to be made and why they were important to our organization. We selected a program that was nationally recognized for its best practice standards and promoted the type of behavioral changes we were seeking. The impact of this decision was three-fold. First, we came to an agreement with our physicians on a mutually acceptable goal that was in line with the shift we wanted to create: the transition from fee for service to population health. Second, we created a common vocabulary for our diverse physician group, which helped mitigate known variations in practice methods. Third, we introduced a single focus of change that produced a ripple of positive effects in our effort to move from volume to value. The result was a successful course correction in the way our physicians delivered care, which benefitted the entire organization.

WELCOME NEW IDEAS

*"Great things in business are never done by one person.
They're done by a team of people."*

—Steve Jobs

ONE OF THE BEST WAYS A VISIONARY LEADER CAN HELP OTHERS is by welcoming their ideas and approaches. The benefit of welcoming new ideas is an exponential increase in possibility. Suppose you are facing a problem in your organization. You may know ten ways to potentially solve that problem. If you ask another person for help, he or she will also have ten ways to potentially solve the problem. Sharing your ideas may reveal some overlap, but putting your heads together could reveal three new solutions neither of you could have come up with alone. One of those new solutions might be better than all ten of your ideas put together. Are you willing to welcome those new ideas, let go of your ego, and recognize that someone else's approach might be better than your own?

If you resist asking for help or advice, you can only draw on your own knowledge and experience. You're living in the realm of "what you know that you know", which is a tiny amount compared to the knowledge that's out there in the universe. By soliciting the support of others, you also demonstrate to people that you have confidence in their ideas. You become known for your openness and willingness to entertain new possibilities, which helps to enlist others in committing to your vision. These interactions also offer the opportunity for you to gain valuable feedback and make sure your team understands the core of the vision you have created.

LEARN
TO ACTIVELY LISTEN

"To effectively communicate, we must realize that we are all different in the way we perceive the world and use this understanding as a guide to our communication with others."

—Tony Robbins

UP TO THIS POINT, I've spent a lot of time on creating your vision, crafting your message, and repeating it often. I don't want to give the impression that you are the only one doing the talking. The best way to lead is not with your lips, but with your ears. If there is one skill I would like to be able to teach every leader, it would be learning to actively listen. Active listening requires curiosity, self-restraint, and genuine interest in the person sitting in front of you.

The process of active listening begins long before the conversation technically starts. The next time you have a meeting set up, walk yourself through this process:

First, identify the goal of the meeting. Is the meeting happening for research, instructional, or negotiation purposes? Think about who called the meeting and the stated purpose to come up with this answer.

Once you know the purpose, determine the best possible outcome of the meeting. Would you like to walk away with more information, a resolved personnel issue, or the beginnings of a new contract?

Then, come up with a list of questions that you will ask during the meeting to reach your best possible outcome. You should be honestly seeking the answers to these questions. By making it your goal to get certain key information, you'll have to listen closely to the responses.

Now you are ready for the meeting to begin.

Have everyone seated and in a comfortable place.

Use small talk to start. Reacquaint yourself with the person and warm up into the relationship a bit before jumping into the content. This sets everyone at ease and prepares each party for the process of listening during the conversation. Make eye contact throughout and consider incorporating some neurolinguistics programming techniques (discussed below).

Create a space that promotes listening. When others are talking, allow them to finish completely. Avoid speaking on top of them. The goal is not to impress people with how smart you are, but to see how smart you can make them feel.

I like to begin the conversation with a series of questions, particularly if the meeting is about some kind of conflict, so the other person has a chance to express his or her opinion. Some things you might ask include:

> What's really going on here?
> What are you concerned about?
> How is that affecting you?
> What's unfair about it?
> What would you like to see done differently?
> Is there anything else?

This final question is critical. I will ask "Is there anything else?" a few times until the other person truly doesn't have anything else to say. That's the first time somebody is ready to listen to you, when he or she is done talking and feel that they have been heard.

Next, I'll allow the person to ask questions of me. Once this person has all the answers he or she needs, I'll continue with questions of my own, and make sure I listen and fully absorb his or her answers.

This structure may shift around depending on the type of meeting you're in. For example, I might ask the other person to begin with any questions for me in certain contexts. In a concept meeting, I might begin with a different set of questions and open the floor for several people to offer responses.

What matters most is that you continue to actively listen to the responses you receive. Let each person speak until he or she is done and acknowledge that individual as a three-dimensional human being in front of you. As a Visionary Leader, you are ultimately responsible for everyone's job performance, not just your own. Create a comfortable environment and let people tell you what they need to be better at their jobs. Remember that you are responsible for the successful outcome of any meeting you hold. Therefore timely preparation for the meeting is imperative. Always develop a strategy for your meetings in advance. I recommend developing a written outline for the meeting that includes a statement of outcome success and the questions that will help you achieve the outcome. Knowing how you think the participants will react and interact with each other also becomes a valuable tool for achieving your strategy. Finally, always make sure the meeting starts with some small talk which reduces tension and shapes the mood and tone for the meeting.

If you really want to know how to enhance communication, pick up *Unlimited Power* by Tony Robbins. In the book, he talks about neurolinguistics programming, which is a valuable tool in learning how people think and make decisions.

My biggest takeaway from reading about neurolinguistics programming (NLP) is that we need to understand how people process and think on a variety of levels. Someone from New York thinks, acts, and responds differently than someone from Alabama. Age, gender, ethnicity, language, regional background: they're all important factors in making us who we are. As a leader, it's important to be able to connect to your employees and to understand their values, belief structures, and how they process and perform their work.

One example from *Unlimited Power* that I love is when Tony Robbins is tasked with teaching pistol shooting to army officers, a skill that is not in his wheelhouse. As research, he spent time with the best marksmen in the army and began to mimic what they were doing: how they spoke, what they believed, how they moved and breathed. He mimicked what he saw and taught these patterns to a random selection of U.S. Army soldiers. Keep in mind that Tony Robbins is not a master marksman himself, but he is a master at identifying and replicating human behavior. You may have already guessed the surprising results of this experiment. By mimicking the behaviors of the master marksmen, the soldiers were able to significantly improve their pistol shooting scores. Even though they did not specifically train their shooting skills, adopting the attitudes and postures of skilled marksmen boosted their confidence as well as their accuracy.

In the past, NLP had a reputation as being manipulative, partly because it was marketed as a series of techniques to enhance sales. However, the real purpose of neurolinguistics programming is to connect with others in a way that emphasizes similarity more than difference. Once you understand who people truly are, you can work with them based on their individual styles. One size doesn't fit all when it comes to leadership styles, and the same applies to styles of communication. You might slightly change your vocabulary or the way you speak to make someone feel more comfortable. On some unconscious level, you already do this. For example, you probably act just a little differently depending on whether you're talking to a friend or a member of your Board of Directors. NLP teaches you to consciously incorporate those slight changes to create a better connection with the person sitting across from you. You might mirror the way your employee is sitting, slow down your speech to match his or her cadence, or even breathe in the same format and pattern as this employee does. These techniques improve communication and build stronger relationships.

The benefits of active listening and NLP go deep into human psychology. When we recognize people have different motivations, incentives, and senses of humor, we can speak directly to who they are and what drives them. As a result, employees tend to listen better and pay more attention. They trust you and feel understood, which is key if you want to enroll them to support and execute your vision.

STRIVE FOR
A CONSISTENT
COMPANY CULTURE

"The behavior of a business's leaders is, ultimately, the behavior of the organization. As such, it's the foundation of the culture."

—Larry Bossidy

IN MY PREVIOUS ORGANIZATION, we worked to ingrain our mission statement so thoroughly into the company culture that any team member would know that his or her primary responsibility was "to provide superior healthcare and an exceptional patient-centered experience." A consistent company culture leverages the positive aspects of peer pressure to help employees perform in a way that moves everybody closer to your organization's goals.

Maintaining a consistent company culture can require the Visionary Leader to make tough choices. If an individual isn't fully on board with the spirit of your organization, you need to have the courage to move him or her out. This demonstrates that you hold your team accountable to their commitments and that you hold yourself personally responsible for maintaining the standards of the company.

Company culture can be difficult to quantify. In healthcare, we rely heavily on Electronic Medical Records (EMR) systems to gather and organize patient information as well as to provide statistical data about an organization's performance. Even though these systems are continually advancing, we are still seeking ways to measure outcomes such as commitment and attitude. These factors are just as critical to quality patient care as excellent clinical outcomes.

Customers perceive quality based on one individual experience at a time. The key to a positive experience is the interaction between the customer and an organization's employee, and positive experiences are closely correlated to an employee's attitude. Therefore, the lowest common denominator for success in any organization is the quality of the interaction between its customers and its employees. Your organization may have thousands of encounters with customers every day, but to become a high-performing organization, you need top decile results. To do that, your company will need to maintain very high customer satisfaction. No matter what business you are in, your success depends on the highest performance at the point of interface with the customer.

As a leader, if you aren't reinforcing the importance of each team member or employee coming to work every day with a positive attitude, then you have missed a critical point of inflection. Most high-level executives have little to do with the one-to-one customer interactions that drive a business. No matter how smart or skilled I was as a healthcare CEO, I wasn't the one dealing with our patients, day in and day out. It wasn't me who was going to make the organization successful, it was the hourly employee who went the extra mile for a patient, stopped to help another team member, or offered assistance to a lost visitor.

When you wrap your mind around the fact that you're not the reason why the organization is running smoothly, you have broken through a barrier that will give you the insight into evolving and maintaining the culture of success. Ultimately, it is the hard-to-grasp qualities, such as engagement between team members and open lines of communication, which contribute to a strong company culture that unifies itself around your vision. As Dr. John Koster says in his book *n=1*, "When you have led organizations through difficult transformations, you have the courage to see things as they really are. You must let go of what you have created in the past to achieve the future."

DEDICATE YOURSELF COMPLETELY TO YOUR CAUSE

"I would rather be a man of conviction than a man of conformity."

—Martin Luther King, Jr.

HUMAN BEINGS ARE SENSITIVE CREATURES, hard-wired to detect phoniness and insincerity. Paying lip service to a vision and a mission is not enough. A Visionary Leader must have a steadfast commitment to his or her ideals and a stalwart belief in a team's ability to achieve them. Dedication to a cause and faith in others can't be faked, and you'll never get your organization to commit by talking about a vision that you, yourself, don't believe in.

The first decision people make about you is whether they trust you or not. If you can gain their trust, you have an opportunity to truly lead. If you cannot gain their trust, moving your vision forward will be a lonely, uphill climb. You need to be wholeheartedly on board with your vision before you ask for commitment from anybody else. The world is run on relationships, which become the first step in building trust, which leads to people's willingness to follow your lead and commit to your vision. Many leaders don't understand that a Visionary Leader must do the inner work required to be worthy of receiving this kind of commitment from his or her team.

—◀○▶—

I'm the first to admit that faking commitment to a cause has never really been an option for me. Even as a boy I was incapable of pretending to support something I didn't believe in. As a result, I had to get accustomed to the risks involved with speaking up.

One example that sticks with me is the "palace revolt" at one of my previous organizations. In the early to mid nineties, I worked for a health system that had recently separated into distinct for-profit and non-profit sectors. My boss, who oversaw the whole system, wanted to sell the non-profit sector off and retain only the for-profit arm. As the person in charge of the non-profit sector, I felt that our work was continuing the original mission of the organization and wanted to sell the for-profit sector instead. I was so outspoken that I thought I might be fired for what I was saying, but keeping quiet and maintaining the status quo wasn't possible for me. Eventually, a new board chairman came in who was open to my ideas. By this time, the organization was hemorrhaging money, and we eventually were able to set up a merger with another company, sell the for-profit arm of the business, and stay afloat.

There's an important difference between fighting for what you believe in and fighting to be right. I deeply admired the man I worked for, but I also deeply believed that his vision for our organization was misguided. A Visionary Leader must be able to parse the difference between acting out of ego and acting out of dedication to his or her cause. The lesson here is to never let your ego get outside of your own personal space.

KEEP THE LINES
OF COMMUNICATION
OPEN

*"When you put together deep knowledge about a subject
that intensely matters to you, charisma happens. You
gain courage to share your passion, and when you do
that, folks follow."*

—Jerry Porras

MAINTAINING OPEN COMMUNICATION on every level within an organization is one of the most critical roles a Visionary Leader plays. In one of my organizations, we chose to call everyone team members, rather than employees or staff, to remind us all that we are always working together and on the same side.

I would often say that every morning a surgery begins in one of our hospitals, but it doesn't really begin there: it begins at the loading dock, where supplies are cross-docked and placed in bins to go to the hospital. One team member is admitting a patient, another is preparing a meal; hundreds if not thousands of activities happen in the space between the loading dock and the operating room. The patient experience may be straightforward, but when you consider the logistics and coordination of all the activities that need to occur, in the right place and at the right time, things suddenly become much more complex. A general rule of thumb is that whenever things look easy or feel seamless, an enormous amount of energy has been expended to provide you with that experience. Making complex procedures look easy is one of the hallmarks of world-class organizations, and teamwork is the most important ingredient in this recipe for success. It is vital that your employees act as a team and realize that no individual job is more important than another. When you are talking about total customer satisfaction, the job of the surgeon is no more important than the guy on the loading dock.

A team is a group of people supporting each other. Teamwork helps you maintain high quality standards and implement organization-wide improvements. Effective coordination reduces costs and boosts efficiency. The overlap of responsibility and oversight that teamwork creates minimizes mistakes. Right before a surgical procedure, for example, the entire team stops and reviews together: right equipment, right patient, right procedure, right surgical site.

Communication is the backbone of successful teamwork. This is not just in terms of how work gets done but also in how a vision is created. The Visionary Leader provides a global vision and then turns the organization loose to refine the process of getting there.

As a leader, I always loved holding town hall meetings with the team members. Every month, I would write a letter called "Continuing the Conversation" that focused on current issues within the organization. We conducted short, impromptu surveys to solicit opinions and held contests to name things. We used social media to take the conversation to our broader community.

The biggest challenge in communication is bringing it from the managers down to the people on the front lines. I am a staunch advocate of leadership development for any organization, partly because this kind of program can build the habits of communication and open conversation right into the fabric of the organization. When you open the discussion to talk about values, quality, and culture, you help your team members and your company continue to grow.

Many organizations focus their leadership development at the middle manager level and above. This approach fails to recognize that a company is successful because of the relationships between its front-line employees and its customers. An effective leadership development and succession planning process should be carried down to the supervisor and even the line staff level. To understand this concept better, read *Securing Your Organization's Future Through Succession Planning and Leadership Development*, which I co-authored with Dr. Kathryn Dies.

INSTILL CONFIDENCE IN OTHERS

"People must know that their ideas will be listened to and, if they have merit, acted upon. If they do, it is possible to mobilize individual creativity on a very broad scale."

—James A. Champy

WHEN PEOPLE FEEL LIKE THEIR IDEAS ARE VALUED, they are more willing to contribute. Instilling confidence in others also helps a Visionary Leader think differently by exposing him or her to a broader range of perspectives and approaches.

Make it a priority to recognize and encourage everyone in your organization on a regular basis. When you walk down the hallway, say hello to every person you encounter. Pay attention to the small things and create simple ways of recognizing work well-done. A hand-written note or email thanking someone for their efforts can make a meaningful difference to your team members.

One way to instill confidence is to consciously create a learning organization. Part of being a learning organization is leaving room for mistakes. If you are teaching new skills, if you are taking risks as an organization to shape a vision for what's next, there will inevitably be errors. Your team must feel like there is a culture of acceptance and learning from mistakes. If they continually fear punishment for getting things wrong, you will never hear their best and most daring ideas.

This is why a Visionary Leader must do so much preparatory work on his or her mindset. You will need to lead by example, admitting when you have made a mistake and acknowledging where there is room for improvement. This creates a permission structure whereby the entire organization can learn from its mistakes, and further perpetuates the positive cycle of encouraging employees to speak and contribute to the overall success of the organization.

RECOGNIZE WHEN NO NEWS MIGHT BE BAD NEWS

"The most important thing in communication is hearing what isn't said."

—Peter Drucker

IT ALWAYS AMAZES ME WHEN LEADERS BRAG about the lack of complaints they get through their employee feedback process. They take such pride in never receiving any complaints that they fail to realize the flimsy premise upon which their assumptions are built. A lack of formal complaints is not necessarily an indication that your employees don't have any grievances. In other words, no news might actually be bad news.

An organization without an open channel for constructive feedback is not living and breathing. Such a company is fundamentally disconnected from the hearts and minds of the people who show up to work for it every day. Its leaders live under a false sense of security.

At the root of this feedback gap is a lack of trust. Employees need to trust their leader before they feel safe enough to speak their minds. Without trust, you get office gossip, department infighting, and high turnover rates. As a Visionary Leader, never forget the courage required for an individual to stand up and say, "I'm unhappy, and here's why."

Recognize that by nature, a feedback process will bring out those individuals who are chronic complainers, for whom no system, method, process, or ideal is ever good enough. There's at least one in every bunch. At the same time, an organization full of people who are afraid or unwilling to speak out indicates a fundamental management problem that needs to be quickly and thoroughly addressed. Remember, those chronic complainers are most likely already voicing their opinions regardless of whether formal feedback channels are available.

When an organization opens its lines of communication, it becomes more productive. Committed team members who feel free to express their opinions will contribute to a strong culture, reinforcing the value of teamwork and a positive attitude. The best behavior-modification tool an organization has is healthy peer pressure. With a strong, committed work force, the complainers and "dead wood" will often be managed out of the organization without much fuss.

KEEP MOVING
THE GOAL LINE
FORWARD

"People need BHAGs – big hairy audacious goals."

—James C. Collins

THOUGHT LEADER JIM COLLINS encourages us all to find the "Big Hairy Audacious Goal" that we're passionate about. How about aiming for zero-harm healthcare? Even though there are several small-scale examples where zero-harm healthcare is possible, it's still a monster of a goal.

When you tackle a goal this big, start by focusing on the areas where your goal is possible or already happening in your organization. Suppose one hospital in your health system had no catheter infections for one quarter. That's one example of zero-harm. Start asking, "How did the nurses do that?" Replicate what you can, iterate, and keep improving. The achievement comes not necessarily from reaching your goal, which you may never do, but from continuously inspiring your organization to be better.

Of course, as the Visionary Leader you must strike a balance with your employees. Pushing too hard and too fast for improvement or failing to provide enough encouragement along the way can create an organizational culture where people feel unsuccessful. Offer plenty of support as you continue to make progress and acknowledge the strides your team has already made.

Above all, make it clear to your employees that you believe in their ability to do great things and they will consistently live up to your expectations.

ENGAGE
THE CRITICAL MASS

*"The tipping point is that magic moment when an idea,
trend, or social behavior crosses a threshold, tips, and
spreads like wildfire."*

—Malcolm Gladwell

IN THE LAST ORGANIZATION I WORKED FOR, I knew that as CEO I wanted
to implement some big changes. The board had hired me to consolidate
their group of hospitals and clinics into a health system, but it was up to
me to decide how that system should look. From day one, I determined
that the health system would become a unified organization rather than a
federation of independent operations. I wanted one chief operating officer
to lead all three divisions and standardize our best practices. You don't
become a top decile performer doing things three different ways.

To implement this restructuring, I needed to have a "critical mass"
of team members on board. The critical mass of change is said to be the
square root of n, where n is the number of employees in the organization. In my situation, we had 26,000 employees, which meant that we
needed the square root of 26,000, or 161 team members, willing to buy
into this vision. When I started out, there was just one person willing
to buy in: me. However, I kept building relationships, explaining the

circumstances, and articulating my vision for taking the organization in a new direction

Achieving this kind of complex, multivariable goal requires constant communication from those team members at the frontline all the way up to the organization's board. Effective Visionary Leaders will tailor their communication style and content based on who they're speaking to. Ask yourself, "Where do I need my board's support, and how often do I need to share updates with them? What do I need to communicate to the leadership team, the work force and the consumers?" This is always about laying the groundwork to build the infrastructure that will support your vision.

Each quarter, I'd talk to the board about what we had done and where I wanted to head next. When we got close to making any big change, I'd move the organization in that direction. When I got resistance, I'd slow down a little. Sometimes, we came to a standstill in one area and focused on making progress somewhere else. In this way, I incrementally, but continually moved the goal line forward to my vision. Eventually, the health system came under the leadership of a single executive. It took a herculean effort to get a critical mass within the organization who were willing to change. Upon reaching that critical mass, I found the calculations were right: the winds started to shift in my direction. From there, things fell into place more quickly until 26,000 of us were finally moving toward the same goal.

DEVELOP LEADERSHIP POTENTIAL

"Winning companies win because they have good leaders who nurture the development of other leaders at all levels of the organization."

—Noel Tichy

ONE OF THE BEST WAYS TO INSTILL THE COMPANY CULTURE you desire is to implement a leadership development program. Succession planning and leadership development are at the heart of nurturing talent in your organization. You are strengthening the strongest, smartest, and most adaptable people you can find, those true-blue team players who are willing to buy in completely to your vision. By offering them the skills they need to flourish and succeed, you gain loyal, lifelong employees. You also create a continually regenerating pool of talent for the executive roles in your company. It's less costly than working with a headhunter and the speed of change is dramatic.

Leadership development turns employees into leaders and helps them liberate their thinking by letting go of the illusion of control. You allow them to create something out of nothing or imagine a new system or method that doesn't yet exist. Dropping ideas at people's feet, which I've talked about in this book, is one example of a highly effective way nurturing talent.

The following paragraphs are excerpted from my book, *Securing Your Organization's Future Through Succession Planning and Leadership Development*, a complete manual for creating and implementing succession planning and leadership development programs in your organization.

> *Developing leaders is about far more than ensuring that the future of the top few spots within the company are secure. Leadership development gives the gifts of innovation and empowerment, helps employees think for themselves, and teaches them how to envision the world in which they want to live. An organization full of leaders benefits far more than the bottom line. Leadership improves and strengthens company culture, and indirectly strengthens the families of those in the organization and even the community at large. A company full of potential CEOs is one of the greatest assets an organization could ever hope to acquire.*
>
> Benefits of Succession Planning and Leadership Development include:
>
> ### Organizational continuity
> *Every company wants a smooth, seamless transition from one CEO to the next. In a best-case scenario, succession planning provides this easy transition by identifying an internal candidate who has been receiving leadership development and is thoroughly prepared to take over the role. One advantage in this type of situation is that the candidate is already familiar with the day-to-day operations of the company. She knows where to find the conference rooms and how to log in to the email system. These considerations may seem minor and temporary, but they eat into the time and energy of a brand-new executive. Additionally, an internal candidate in succession planning will have been preparing for the specific challenges of a new role for the past 6-18 months, with the opportunity to observe and*

work closely with the current CEO, giving her a real sense of what the position entails.

Maintaining company culture

Aside from smoothly maintaining daily operations and minimizing the technical onboarding process, the board should consider the advantages that an internal candidate might offer with respect to maintaining company culture. Many (although not all) organizations today spend a significant amount of energy on developing the company's mission, vision, and core values, which can overall be described as the company culture. There is tremendous effort put forth to infuse these ideas from the top of the organization to the bottom, so that each employee not only understands the company culture but embraces and fully lives it as well. In this way, you make company culture a part of the organization's DNA.

An external candidate will require additional time to understand your company culture in a fully integrated way. He may agree with the mission, vision, and values in theory, but his actions may not reflect alignment with these ideas; perhaps he does not agree with some of the values at all. No amount of rigorous interviewing can fully predict an individual's behavior once he enters the workplace. The process of hiring an external candidate is simply no match for the daily observation of internal candidates in a succession planning program, where these candidates are coached and trained specifically in accordance with the company culture.

Cascading effect

Employee retention is a huge motivator for organizations to institute succession planning and leadership development programs. When a key leadership position is filled by an in-

dividual who already works for the company, the employee retention extends beyond that individual. If an executive at level C ascends to a position at level B, there is now an open spot in level C management. It is highly likely that a candidate at level D will be prepared to take over that position, leaving an opportunity in level D for a leader from level E to step into, and so on. Filling one position internally creates a sequence of other available roles. There is a cascading effect throughout the entire company when an internal candidate is promoted. Other employees now see that there is plenty of opportunity for growth; in turn, they work harder to become better leaders. A successful succession planning program increases employee retention and improves job satisfaction throughout an entire organization.

Ability to plan ahead

Even if you determine that a position cannot be filled by an internal promotion, the tools of succession planning can still prepare an organization for the departure of key leaders. Monies can be allocated to a budget for an external search in advance. Arrangements can be made for other leaders to cover certain vital responsibilities of the departing executive until the position has been filled. Occasionally, the role of a key leader needs to be reimagined or redefined due to shifts in the organization or in the industry. Succession planning allows your company to anticipate those changes, so that when the time comes for hiring, even externally, you are crystal clear as to the specific qualifications that the next candidate must possess.

Financial repercussions

There are two main ways in which succession planning reduces costs to an organization, which you can highlight as you move forward with your program.

First, you save the company costly searches for external candidates. When a high-level executive is hired from the outside, the placement or executive search firm that will be involved collects a hefty fee, generally the equivalent of 30% of the individual's new salary. Think about the salaries for the top five executives in your company. This amount is easily tens of thousands, and often hundreds of thousands of dollars in finder's fees alone. Although this is the single largest expenditure for hiring a new candidate, there are other costs to the process as well.

Beyond agency fees, your organization must pay travel expenses for all external candidates during the interview process, including airfare, hotel stays, and transportation. Once a candidate has been selected, you will also be expected to pay for his relocation. Occasionally an organization will get lucky and can hire an external candidate who is already local, but the higher up the ladder you go, the less likely this becomes.

The second way in which succession planning reduces an organization's costs is more difficult to quantify but has important implications. When you bring an external candidate into a high-level position in a company, it takes a lot longer for him to get up to speed than an internal candidate. Any change in CEO, for example, will disrupt the flow of business and alter social dynamics, but the dust settles a lot faster with an internal candidate who has a firm grasp on company values and culture, and the course of daily operations.

USE TECHNOLOGY TO BRIDGE THE GENERATIONAL GAP

"While technology is important, it's what we do with it that truly matters."

—Muhammad Yunus

A VISIONARY LEADER IS WILLING TO LOOK AT THE YOUNG PEOPLE in his or her organization and able to recognize that the future lies with them. Millennials differ from their predecessors in many ways, but their most notable departures have to do with their relationship to technology.

I look at healthcare in much the same way my parents did. When I get sick, I go to the doctor to see what is wrong with me. When my millennial-age daughter gets sick, she hops online to look for a diagnosis. Then, she goes to a doctor-rating service to find a specialist compatible with her self-diagnosis before making an appointment. In some places, she can chat with a physician right over the computer and pick up her prescription from the local pharmacy an hour later. It's a different world today, and all industries and markets need to recognize the evolving needs and expectations of their consumers.

My daughter owns a smartphone, but I joke that she doesn't know what the second half of that word means. For a long time, I refused to adapt. I would call and call and call, and she never picked up the phone, rarely called

me back. If I sent her a text message, however, she'd respond almost immediately. So, I learned to text. I don't see this as inherently good or bad. It's
simply the way of the world, and we can choose to adapt and succeed—like
the duck-billed platypus—or resist and perish.

PART V

EXECUTING
THE VISION

I WANT TO NOTE SOMETHING IMPORTANT about the structure of this book. The nature of reading is that it lays out a clear linear path, one page after another. It may seem that the journey of a successful Visionary Leader is equally clear and linear: one first completes all the mindset and personal transformation work, then moves on to tackle the Success Formula in a neat, sequential order. The process isn't nearly as tidy when it's applied in the real world. It is true that you need to prepare your mind before you are ready to create a vision. It is also true, however, that you'll continue to learn about yourself while you're engaged in the Success Formula. Being a Visionary Leader is not step-by-step; it's additive. It's like juggling, where each phase is another ball you have to keep up in the air. You've finished reading the section "Committing to the Vision", but that phase is far from over. Commitment is ongoing at all times, regardless of how close or far your organization is from reaching its goals. You must continue to build and maintain strong relationships with your team and keep re-enrolling them to support the picture of the future that's living inside your head.

The final phase is really where the rubber meets the road. It's time to dive into "Executing the Vision".

LEARN TO PARTITION YOUR MIND

"The mind can only see what it is prepared to see."

—Edward de Bono

To simultaneously be the leader of your organization as it is today and put your company on a trajectory toward the future, you need to develop the skill of partitioning your mind. The mindset work in the first part of this book will clear the path for you to accomplish this by de-cluttering your conscious thoughts and allowing your subconscious mind to produce more solutions.

When you partition your mind, you strengthen your vision. I've talked about the need for a vision that is so clear that you can go out and walk around in it. You should be able to mentally explore the landscape that you have created, see your success in living color, and envision what operating in that environment feels and looks like. Once you have a clear grasp on your vision, you'll be able to articulate the infrastructure needed to get there. Seeing the future laid out before you makes it easier to understand the nature and timing of the complex changes required to be successful in that future.

If you can think about what is important today, next quarter, eighteen months from now, and ten years down the road, you can match resources and infrastructure needs to this rolling forecast. This will prepare you for the organization's inevitable evolution. A Visionary Leader needs to know the eventual destination, but also needs to understand the route to get there. Holding the future and the present in the same moment continuously reinforces to your team the importance of their role in executing your vision.

Be aware that your vision may be multiple degrees different from your original picture when you reach it. To understand what I mean, think about the process of filming a movie. There's a huge team of people working on a single film, with each person offering a unique contribution to create the finished product. The director's cut of a movie often looks quite different from the final cut audiences see in theaters. This is why people who achieve their goals often say, "The final version doesn't look much like my initial vision—but it feels right."

GET A FIRM GRIP ON JELL-O

"Ideas are elusive, slippery things."

—Earl Nightingale

HOW DO YOU GET A FIRM GRIP ON JELL-O? If you hold too tightly or squeeze too hard, it will slide right out from underneath you. The answer is that to get a firm grip really requires a soft touch. This is the same kind of alert but relaxed energy you see with professional athletes. If they hold the bat or the golf club too tightly, if they try to exert too much force or control, excellence eludes them.

Leading is a lot like holding onto Jell-O. Your company might face serious challenges in the marketplace. You may be fully aware that you don't have the resources or talent you need. Perhaps your competitors have an edge or are farther ahead. Even so, you can't clamp down in your desire for control. If you squeeze too hard, success, like the Jell-O, will always elude you. Instead, you've got to take a softer approach to change and move the organization forward. Incidentally, this lighter touch will keep you flexible instead of rigid, allowing you to navigate obstacles more easily.

Acknowledge those moments when you have a long way to go in a short amount of time. Figure out how you're going to get from point A to point B with the best results possible. The best results possible may not be perfect. Learn to accept it.

To lead a group of people, you must be gentle, but firm. Help your team understand the objective and what each individual needs to contribute to reach it. Offer whatever resources and support you can to fulfill their needs so they can meet the objective. Recognize that you can't grab hold of your vision and grasp it tightly, but that you need a light, cool touch instead.

Most importantly, using a light touch doesn't mean giving up the intensity of your focus when facing difficult times or major challenges. Be gentle, but make it clear that in the face of adversity, you will not give up, but are instead prepared to redouble your efforts. At this point, you must constantly reinforce the soundbites you have created to explain your vision, accelerate the frequency of updates from your leadership team, and keep communication channels open with your board.

INTEGRATE INFRASTRUCTURE INTO YOUR VISION

"Stop setting goals. Goals are pure fantasy unless you have a specific plan to achieve them."

—Stephen Covey

I ONCE WORKED FOR A MAN who was constantly working on the latest, greatest plan to transform his organization. Every time we had a problem he would go away for a week and come back with a new scheme. This usually involved reorganizing the system, changing everybody's position, and passing responsibilities back and forth. No one could remember his or her own job title, and no one knew who was supposed to oversee what. In short, our heads were spinning.

Vision without infrastructure is like words without sentences. Without the support of a sentence structure, all the words in the world won't ever add up to a single idea.

It takes more than a great vision to lead people to success. To transform your vision into reality, you must be able to walk people through a process to get there as well. You need to spend time and energy understanding the infrastructure that your ideas will require, and you need a comprehensive sense of what pieces need to be in place before you can even come close to realizing your vision. Then, you need to gather the appropriate resources and hire the right people to help you achieve it. As a Visionary Leader, you must become an expert at execution.

Working against the status quo and outside an organization's comfort zone is difficult, and, as we have seen, the Visionary Leader may be the only person convinced that moving in a certain direction will lead the organization to a better place—at least at first. Do not underestimate the potential for resistance and the length of time required to get buy-in from your key leadership team. To be successful, you must secure the commitment of those key leaders who will bring your new vision to life and garner support from the team members who are doing the daily work to help you achieve it. Inspiring people to commit means changing their thinking one mind at a time.

When it comes to executing a vision, you want to be Julian Schnabel, not Evil Knievel. There is always more than one way to solve a problem, particularly when transitioning to a new business model requires crossing a massive gap in knowledge, culture, technology, or industry. Crossing the gap between the present and the future is often a Visionary Leader's greatest challenge. The bold move is to try to jump the gap like Evil Knievel. The risk is that if your jump is a little too short, it's a long way down.

I recommend the Julian Schnabel approach instead. Gather your resources, create a design, and construct a bridge to cross the gap. While this method is no doubt longer and more tedious, it's also a sturdier, safer option that guarantees your entire organization will make it to the other side.

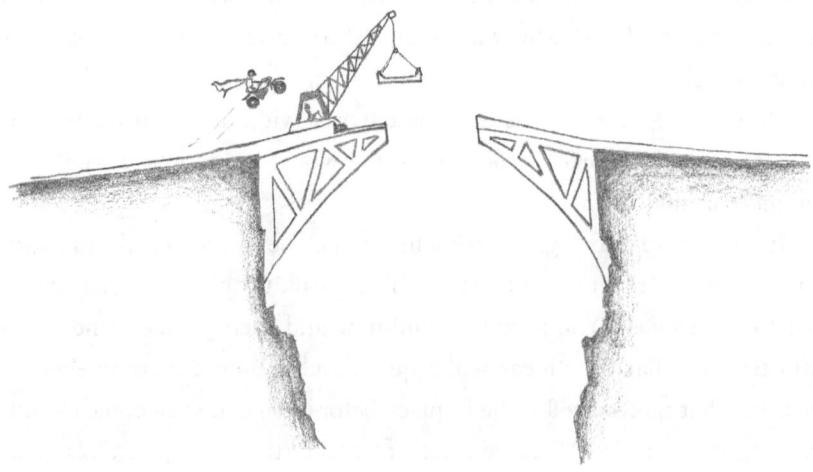

You build your bridge by laying careful plans to avoid a cataclysmic disruption in the existing business while you shift to a new model. This is what it means to create meaningful infrastructure in an organization, and it takes time, dedication, and planning. Investing in efficiency, streamlining processes, and incorporating new technology are all measures that will help an organization endure for years to come.

In healthcare, there is no more archetypal example of infrastructure than Electronic Medical Records (EMR). Organizations need EMR systems to help them measure superior outcomes. They do this by systemizing an enormous amount of data that previously had to be manually extracted from patient records. Before EMR, nurses had to review charts one by one, looking for certain data points or patterns. This was time-consuming enough, but there was a bigger problem: they could only look for what they'd been asked to review. If other factors came under consideration, they had to go back and review thousands of patient charts again to look for new data points. EMR provides organizations unprecedented access to data which can be quickly sifted to make connections between specific factors and linked outcomes. It is almost impossible to reach top decile performance in healthcare without a data management system that is robust enough to allow for the evaluation of data at the individual user level.

In the last organization I worked for, we knew we needed to implement an EMR system in order to move toward one of our big goals, zero-harm healthcare. Our projected timeline was five to seven years, and we ended up taking the full seven years to complete the project. This was a long, winding journey, not without its setbacks, but EMR was critical infrastructure we needed to have in place. Our ability to measure data would have been so limited without it that moving toward zero-harm healthcare would have been not just an audacious goal, but an impossible one. Needless to say, this was a long, winding journey. Having the infrastructure in place was critical because we could not realistically talk about achieving our vision until we had successfully implemented our EMR. Not every piece of infrastructure will require a timeline this lengthy, but if you run a large organization, you should expect that some of your transitions will take longer to thoroughly execute than you would like.

The key to everyone keeping their sanity during an ongoing effort of this magnitude is communication. Each time we rolled out a new phase of the EMR implementation, we examined our relationships with patients as well as with team members. We made sure that the process continually allowed us to improve the experience of our patients, and we also anticipated and received feedback regarding the needs of our employees as their roles continued to evolve. Continuous evaluation of your progress during a major execution phase is vital to keeping your vision on course.

ANTICIPATE
THE NEEDS OF
YOUR STAFF IN ADVANCE

"Dig your well before you're thirsty."

—Seth Godin

CHANGE DOES NOT HAPPEN IN A VACUUM. A strong vision will touch every member of your organization, and this kind of shifting can create fear and uncertainty among your employees. As a Visionary Leader, you are responsible for considering the ways in which the lives of your team members will be affected by the vision you seek to bring forth.

I mentioned an organizational switch to an Electronic Medical Records system in the last chapter, and I mentioned how that process took a full seven years to implement. We had to go slowly so that we could anticipate the needs of our staff and the ways in which they would be affected by this transition. During this process, somebody on my team was thoughtful enough to recognize that by switching from paper records to electronic, every record-keeping process we had would subsequently need to change. So, we looked at which team members were at the greatest risk of being frustrated, angry, or upset by this transition. Incidentally, these were the same people who we most needed to be committed to the EMR system's success: nurses. Medical records begin at the nursing station, and our nursing staff was going to experience a big shift in some aspects of their jobs once EMR was implemented. For EMR to succeed, it was vital that we addressed the needs and expectations of these individuals.

To do this, we started by significantly increasing the budget for the EMR implementation. All our nurses had to undergo training to learn the new system, which could leave our nursing stations short-staffed. We made sure to pay for temporary coverage whenever one nurse had to be out for training. In the end, we spent less than half of what we budgeted. When people realized that the organization was committed to thorough EMR training, they didn't always ask for extra staff coverage when a nurse was out learning the new system. However, they always appreciated knowing that they had extra support available if they needed it.

Although the process of EMR implementation did temporarily disrupt the nursing staff's daily routine, the nurses themselves were as vital to our organization as ever. Still, as we continued implementing this system, we became aware of another group of our team members whose positions were in jeopardy.

Before EMR, we worked from paper patient records. Two of our hospitals previously had massive storage rooms manned by medical records clerks who filed and maintained these records. Once the transition to EMR was complete, there would no longer be a need for paper medical records clerks within our organization. Yet, these individuals were essential in making sure the EMR transition ran smoothly and on-time. We were faced with a serious question: how do we get employees to commit to a program whose success will leave them without a position in the company?

We wanted to help those clerks transition to new positions, not just to avoid any sabotage of the process, but because we were dedicated to their growth and development as individuals. It's part of the responsibility of a learning organization. With the help of a local college, we created an informatics course and gave all our clerks the opportunity to enroll. This course taught them the necessary skills to take on a different role in the organization, one related to the new EMR system. For individuals who didn't want the informatics course, we looked for opportunities to cross-train them into other positions in the company. By directly acknowledging people's concerns about job security and offering other alternatives for positions within the organization, we helped people become more comfortable with the inevitable shift in the status quo.

To alleviate fear, you need to help people understand their role in the organization's future and then help them get there. When you anticipate the needs of your team members, you demonstrate you care about their well-being, which instills deep confidence and loyalty. As a Visionary Leader, you're often standing on the hill to get a view of the future from above. However, you need to make sure you also have people on the ground to identify the kind of granular changes that affect real people within your organization.

You are not solely responsible for anticipating and building out every detail of the execution phase. Rather, you need to hire the right people and listen to what they say. Understand enough about the infrastructure that you can walk other people through an overview of what a project will require. Your employees won't be looking to your systems experts or your consultants for what to do next; they'll be looking to you.

PREPARE
FOR A MARATHON,
NOT A MAD DASH

*"Most people overestimate what they can do in one year
and underestimate what they can do in ten years."*

—Bill Gates

MANY ORGANIZATIONS WILL REACH A GOAL by putting in a big effort very quickly, only to find that they are unable to sustain their results for any significant length of time. There is no doubt that most organizations can temporarily improve their performance through a tremendous burst of effort, but short-term improvements don't always translate into long term success. A Visionary Leader looks for success over a long period of time, year after year. This kind of longevity requires a culture of people who are continually focused on the company's mission as a way of acting out your vision. This is at the heart of why creating and implementing infrastructure is so critical. Otherwise, what you see in your head will remain where it is and never become a reality.

Let's look at one last aspect of my experience implementing an Electronic Medical Records (EMR) system. When I arrived in May 2004, the game plan was to bring the board a $180M request to develop an EMR system for the organization.

A month into my tenure, it dawned on me how poorly equipped we were to begin this process. I terminated the head of our IT department and two weeks later, terminated four directors and two managers. I brought in an interim department head and three directors who were supervised by an outside information services firm. Their primary goal was to help us build a credible Information Systems (IS) department, which had to be in place before we could even think about implementing an EMR system.

At the time, the Computer Center for the IS Department was in a windowed building that overlooked a retention pond. When you stood at the back door that led to the outside, you could see the retention pond fifteen yards away. When you looked to your right, there were three steps that led down to a room where all the battery back-ups were stored in case the power went out.

I visited this room and noticed a pile of sandbags sitting next to the door. When I asked what they were for, I was told that when it rained, the retention pond would flood and water would run under the door. The sandbags were to prevent the water from seeping into the building. This was literally ten feet away from the stairs that led to the backup batteries for the hospital system information services.

The greatest vision in the world will never get you where you want to go if you're in this kind of situation.

So, I decided we needed a year off. We had to get our IS situation in order, and our new goal was to have the EMR system up and running in five years.

In total, it took us seven years instead of five, and we spent $320M, not $180M. That was before acquiring the algorithms and knowledge we needed to turn our data into real, usable information to produce state-of-the-art patient outcomes.

EMR implementation isn't an anomaly either. Our Succession Planning and Leadership Development program took eight years to get to a place where it was fully functioning, measurable, and integrated into the organizational culture. It took a full nine years to consolidate the management of the organization so that all the operating officers reported to one person. I started that project my very first day as CEO.

What happens if you try to implement too quickly? You'll make mistakes and underestimate how long it's going to take. You'll forget to account for the impact of the changes and the pushback you might get from employees.

There's a health system that took to heart the switch from volume to value that I've mentioned several times throughout this book. They correctly identified where the future was headed and they wanted to be the leader in the field. So, their entire leadership team skillfully implemented a value-based system and completely decimated their entire revenue stream in the process.

You can have all the right ideas, but if you move too soon or too quickly, you're likely to fail.

Why does fast, drastic change often have spectacularly disastrous results? In the case of brand new leadership, it's usually because the leader doesn't yet understand how the organization works. He or she is likely trying to replicate something from the past that was effective without acknowledging the differences between the current organization and the previous one. Even a Visionary Leader must slip into the stream and paddle alongside everybody else at first. Learn how the currents move and who else is in the water with you. Then, you can move to the front and direct the paddling.

The second reason dramatic change is ineffective is that it fails to recognize that meaningful change comes from shifting the hearts and minds of real human beings within the organization. People are risk-averse by nature and prefer to maintain the status quo, even if the status quo isn't functioning optimally. It's a classic case of choosing the "devil you know" over the "devil you don't". For an organization to make effective and significant changes, its employees must have unfailing trust in its leadership. Building trust, opening lines of communication, understanding where employees are coming from and how change will affect their lives: this all takes time, especially when scaled to teams of thousands of employees.

Your vision must consider the reality of what kind of effort you'll put in, walls you must walk through, and what else you haven't thought of that needs to occur. My recommendation is to develop a strategy, set the timeline, and then double the amount of time required for the initial relationship-building phase. If there isn't an alignment of culture and values, the path forward will be rocky. Never try to push too hard or too fast against hesitation.

Never justify skipping a step of integration by vowing to implement it later. All parties need to be on board for change to even have a chance at success.

Some organizational changes are extensive. Some need to be done sequentially. Some are iterative. This gets back to the idea of partitioning your mind. Part of you needs to go into the new space of your vision and ask yourself questions from that new space. Part of you needs to be grounded in the current realities of the organization.

The question you must ask is: "How do I get brand new results with the tools I have available right now?"

The answers will be different from the way things have always been done. That's innovation and creativity. That's looking around the corner.

You must evaluate your situation according to its own circumstances. Not every organization will have the ideal money, resources, and leadership to move forward. You must start from where you are. See what cards you've been dealt and play your hand from there. You already have everything you need to succeed, even if the creative solutions that will lead you to success have yet to reveal themselves. Access to resources does make things easier, but I've seen organizations with nothing—literally in bankruptcy—work their way back from financial ruin. It's more than possible. Any organization can succeed if it has a clear vision, a committed leadership team, a strong company culture, a plan for execution, and the willingness to do whatever necessary to accomplish its goals.

I like to think of an organization as a cruise ship that needs plenty of open water to make a turn. In big organizations, change takes a long time. Leave yourself plenty of room to make the shift or the pivot and try to keep a 360° view as often as possible. As the leader, it's your job to be continuously evaluating the directional shifts you need and to adjust your plan accordingly to make the turn.

KEEP YOUR MISSION AS YOUR GUIDE

"If everything is important, then nothing is."

—Patrick Lencioni

IN AN EARLIER CHAPTER, I said that your mission should act as your compass. If your vision is your destination, then your mission is the tool which tells you whether you are still headed in the right direction. Organizations with bold, simple, straight-line missions consistently have the greatest success. In knowing exactly what they want, they can get very clear about the most effective steps to achieve their goals. Running a large organization gets very complex, very fast. Your mission will always help you navigate the maze.

Not every organization's mission is to create revolutionary change in the world. I have a friend who started working in a tire store when he was young. The owner saw promise in him and helped him start a business of his own. My friend took that first opportunity and ran with it. His vision was to provide high-quality sales and service for tires, and to open 500 locations nationwide, and that's exactly what he did.

What made him so successful was that he knew exactly who he was selling to: the average guy driving a Ford Pinto. He didn't get distracted by what his competitors were doing or by seemingly more lucrative "opportunities" that would have veered his business off-course. My friend knew he wasn't there to sell fancy, expensive tires; he was there to sell reliable tires at a reasonable price. He made sure to offer great service and good discounts and ran a smart marketing campaign to boot.

This story ties together many of the concepts I've discussed throughout this book. First and foremost, my friend took an opportunity that was laid at his feet and ran with it. He created a vision that was clear and stayed the course in his commitment to that vision. Once he began to be successful, he didn't become distracted, try to change his brand, or up level too soon. He systematically executed his vision, and along the way, he made sure to provide a high level of service toward his client, the average Joe driving the Ford Pinto.

My friend ended up selling each of his 500 tire stores for $500,000. From there, he invested his $250 million in car dealerships and now generates around $160 million per quarter.

At the end of the day, any leader can be a Visionary Leader. Your vision doesn't have to disrupt the entire market or change the face of the industry forever. It just needs to be deeply meaningful to you.

Ask for help
when you need it

*"Ask for help not because you're weak, but because you
want to remain strong."*

—Les Brown

When you're the CEO, you don't really do much project work. Your direct
impact on customers or clients is minimal. Every day, you rely on your employees to effectively handle those customer or client interactions. Your team
members are critical to the success of the organization. At the same time,
very few companies are purely employee-run and leaderless. An organization
with a strong leader, who has great vision and relationships with his or her
team and inspires the team to lead with the mission and vision in mind, will
demonstrate the path to success.

As CEO of the company, your role is to set the tone for the organization's culture and to nurture and develop your leadership team. Never forget
that every single day, you're asking for their help. Your employees at all levels
are carrying the torch of your organization's message out into the world. Acknowledging how much help you need is humbling. It protects you from
your own ego and transforms the way you interact with your employees.
You simply can't do it without them.

—◀〇▶—

I've always found that anytime I reached out for help, I received 110 percent of people's efforts and assistance. When I was finishing my residency, my preceptor left the health system, making me one of two masters-trained individuals in Health Administration. The other guy was Russ Miller, the Executive Vice President of Administration. One day, he called me into his office and said to me, "I need you to meet with all of the department heads and help them. See me if you have a problem."

I was a brand-new graduate, standing before a man who was asking me to take on a leadership role for a health system with over 500 beds. I felt like I was standing on the edge at the deep end of the pool and didn't know how to swim. I asked, "Where do I start?"

Russ was a great big guy, red-faced, and when he shook your hand, you thought it had disappeared into a pillow. He chewed cigars, but didn't smoke them. He'd been chewing a cigar as he was talking to me, but now he deliberately took the cigar out of his mouth.

"I want you to go out there and help these department heads, and if you have a problem, come back and see me. Do I have to say that a third time?"

I hardly made a splash as he shoved me into the water.

Back in my little cubicle, I sat there, staring at the wall and asking myself: what do I do now? The first thing I thought of was to make a list of key department heads, go to each one individually, and confess everything. One by one, I approached them and was brutally honest: "Russ has given me a huge responsibility. I'm not capable of doing the job, but it's what he's asked me to do. I don't have the experience to work my way through this alone. Can you help me?"

Help me is exactly what each one of them did. Those department heads helped me do my job and made me look good while doing it. They supported me and covered for me. They kept me in the loop about what they were doing and gave me a heads up when there was something I needed to know.

I brought them my problems and they offered solutions. That's when it really hit home for me: leadership is a team sport, not a solo competition. It's not about proving you're better or smarter than your employees; it's about recognizing their talent and skills and being so confident in yourself that you can rely on them to make your organization a success.

CREATE CLEAR STANDARDS AND BEST PRACTICES

"Make compliance policies and procedures comprehensible to mere mortals."

—Jeff Grimshaw and Gregg Baron

IF AN EMPLOYEE KNOWS EXACTLY WHAT IS EXPECTED of him or her, he or she has a much greater chance of meeting that expectation. A Visionary Leader establishes expectations by creating clear standards and best practices that align with the organization's core mission.

We've discussed how important it is that when you craft a message for your organization, you keep it simple. Each employee will internalize your message slightly differently based on their own personal filter of unique life experiences. This differentiation is inevitable, because people are people, but it's also an asset because it adds more brainpower and creativity into the process of making your vision a reality.

However, as the Visionary Leader, you want to ensure that these inspired actions your employees are taking based on their own unique interpretations of your message don't go too far afield. Enter clear standards and best practices, which are guidelines and measures to help you keep all the pieces and people of your organization moving in the same direction.

Let's look at an example of four key results that I helped set up in accordance with the vision for an organization:

- *Superior patient experience.* High levels of customer service and patient satisfaction.
- *One standard of care.* Systematizing policies and procedures for a company with over 23,000 employees and 300 patient access points.
- *Top decile performance.* Consistently ranking in the top 10 percent of health systems in the country.
- *Financial stability.* Being able to afford it all. This is really the by-product of wisely selecting the other key results.

These results areas gave employees guardrails and helped guide them when they were making decisions on the job. We provided employees with plenty of information about these key results areas and helped them understand how their individual positions contributed to the organization's success. By defining boundaries for our team, we were able to further streamline our operations and continue our trajectory of growth and evolution.

GUARD THE TRUST
OTHERS PLACE IN YOU

"The toughest thing about the power of trust is that it's
very difficult to build and very easy to destroy."

—Thomas J. Watson

IN THE COMMITMENT PHASE OF THE SUCCESS FORMULA, I talked about the importance of helping every member of your organization understand and take ownership of your vision. As a Visionary Leader, you must build relationships, foster collaboration, and allow individuals to internalize the core message of your vision in their own unique ways. I want to emphasize again that engaging your team does not end once you move to the Execution phase. Reinforcing your team's commitment is an ongoing process that continues to be vital to the health and success of the organization. People need to feel listened to and respected 100 percent of the time, not just when you are seeking their participation or support.

Trust is hard to build and easy to lose. The vast majority of conflict in organizations comes from misunderstandings borne out of poor communication. One person makes a remark that somebody else takes the wrong way, and boom! Instant conflict. The end result is a breakdown in trust, which takes considerable time and effort to rebuild once it has been lost.

At the heart of a successful organization is a strong company culture, and at the core of a strong company culture is trust. This is why relationships and relationship-building are necessary to be a successful leader. Most communities and organizations are very diverse. We vary in age, race, gender, religion, and national heritage, with different belief structures, societal norms, and values. Some of us are raised in different geographies and in rural or urban settings. English may not be our first language.

As a leader, it becomes your responsibility to lead people to inclusiveness by encouraging them to get to know their co-workers. People don't have to change their beliefs, but they do need to get to understand how the people they work with think and process situations through their own unique experiences. It's important to build an organizational culture that honors and respects every culture and belief that team members encounter. When you create this kind of environment, based on understanding and mutual respect, you not only gain the trust of your employees, but you create the conditions wherein they learn to deeply trust one another as well.

UNDERSTAND
THAT WE PROCESS
THINGS DIFFERENTLY

*"Managers must have the discipline not to keep pulling
up the flowers to see if their roots are healthy."*

—Robert Townsend

BY THE TIME I RETIRED AS CEO of my last organization, I didn't even write a letter by myself. Someone from communications would sit down with me, and I'd tell him or her what I wanted to write about. We'd talk about it for fifteen minutes and then later that day, I'd have the draft of the letter on my desk. That's because the folks in communications are much better at writing than I am. My job wasn't to write the best letter possible; it was to lead the organization and focus on its role in the community, state, and nation. You should be the keeper of your vision, but you should not try to execute every aspect of it yourself.

One common leadership mistake is something I often see with a new manager that is what I call, "doing watch repair with heavy gloves". Doing watch repair with heavy gloves describes the feeling you get when, as a leader, you watch an employee struggle with a skill or task that is second nature to you. It would feel clunky to fix a watch while wearing gloves instead of using your bare hands. Guiding employees, helping them learn, and allowing them to make mistakes can also feel awkward, frustrating, and inefficient. Nevertheless, it's vital that manager and employee both be allowed to move through this process, slow and painful as it may be, for them to develop and grow.

Here's a second example: suppose you are a frequent baker and have a signature cake you love to bake. You can bake this cake in your sleep: the recipe is memorized, you know how much you need of each ingredient, and you can move through the whole process quickly and efficiently. Now, suppose you are telling somebody else how to bake the cake, someone who has very little experience in the kitchen. This is the discomfort young managers often feel with newer employees. It would be easier in the short term to snatch the mixing bowl and measuring cup and just do it yourself; in the long run, however, the inexperienced baker will be no better off than when he or she started.

Instead of allowing that individual the time and space to find his or her own process, new managers often get frustrated and start micro-managing. A classic indication that you're in this cycle is the thought, *Nobody else can do it the right way, I'll just do it myself*. Micro-managing undermines your employees' self-confidence, diminishes their trust in you, and stifles the creativity and innovation that comes from having other voices and opinions in the room.

A Visionary Leader gets the best results by giving capable and talented people a concept or a problem and letting them come up with their own solution. Your responsibility is to keep your team focused on the mission and to sustain the vision so that they never forget what they are working toward. When you see an employee coming up with a solution that is not ideal or not the way you would have done it, resist the impulse to micromanage. You become a true leader by going through that uncomfortable process of instructing employees without interfering in their process.

If you can learn to allow others to have their own process, you will increase their level of dedication to the organization. You will boost self-confidence and instill passion, pride, and a sense of accomplishment. You will gain more trust by giving it, and you will add one more individual to the dedicated army of your organization.

ACKNOWLEDGE THE PROS AND CONS OF COMPETITION

"The essence of competitiveness is liberated when we make people believe that what they think and do is important—and then get out of their way while they do it."

—Jack Welch

NEVER BE AFRAID TO COMPETE. A healthy sense of competition keeps you focused on building a high-performing organization. Competition breeds disruptive technologies and innovation in system processes. It makes you stronger and more current in your line of business. Competition causes good organizations to become great by keeping them just outside the comfort zone of business as usual.

It is important to know your competition thoroughly. Put yourself in the shoes of your competition to understand their mission, sales process, values infrastructure, pricing, etc. Understanding how they think, what their strengths are, and where they are weak can be incredibly helpful, particularly in those head-to-head situations.

On the other hand, there are many instances where an undue focus on competition isn't healthy. I see unnecessary competition in the spiteful way that organizations sometimes view each other, constantly trying to outperform and outmaneuver their peers in the industry. The reality is that even similar organizations have substantial differences, and anti-trust laws all but guarantee that no one company will end up with 100 percent of the market.

Obsessing over your competition is not healthy. You need to acknowledge your competitors and work to understand them, but keep your primary focus on your own vision for the future, not theirs. Remember that you can't control the competition. Any efforts to do so are simply buying into an illusion.

A healthy approach is to put your own organization in a place where the competition wakes up every morning and wonders what you're going to do next. If you focus on everything I talk about in this book, you will soon understand that you don't really need to know where you stand against the competition. The best indicator of success is the quality of your customer relationships.

In his book, *The Different Drum: Community Making and Peace*, M. Scott Peck talks about community-forming and the challenge of excess organization in industry, government, and education. He speaks of pure community being devoid of organization and focused instead on the formation of relationships and the understanding of one another so we can be more effective in confronting and dealing with issues collectively. I have always tried to get my leadership teams and the people who work with them more focused on honoring and celebrating each individual's beliefs and culture. The more we can relate to one another, the more effective we can be at setting high standards for our organization and setting goals for teams to achieve those standards. If we pursue seemingly unattainably high standards, there is no room for worrying about what the competition is doing. There is only time to compare where we are in the pursuit of our goals in comparison with the overall industry.

It's healthy to want to improve and to create challenges that help people better focus on what they're trying to accomplish. Yet, on some level, every organization in your industry should be on the same side when it comes to community and national policy that will improve the industry's safety, effectiveness, and service to its customers.

Throughout my career, I had the opportunity to be involved in and chair many industry and civic organizations that were focused on the overall improvement of efforts in the community and nation. When I reflect on the balance between competition and cooperation or coopetition, which is defined as "the practice where competitors work with each other on project-to-project, joint venture or co-marketing basis", I clearly see the value in working at a higher community level, which is above the competitive level and focuses more on the common good of the people the industry serves or the common needs of the industry itself, in order to compete with another industry on the national level. An example of this for me has been the regulation battles between the insurance and health care industries that affect the way patients are cared for and the cost of that care. These efforts always required the joint effort of many organizations in the industry, despite the fact that these organizations competed with one another on a daily basis.

TURN YOUR LANDING LIGHT ON— AND MAYBE OFF AGAIN

"If you can walk away from a landing, it's a good landing."

—Chuck Yeager

BACK WHEN I WAS IN FLIGHT SCHOOL, I heard about one particularly spooky situation. It's known as an "engine out, off-runway landing at night", which is code for crash landing your plane in the dark. Anyway, if this circumstance arises, there is a specific protocol the pilot must follow:

First, try to restart the engine. Second, turn your transponder to the emergency frequency. Third, communicate on the radio your location and your situation. Fourth, turn your landing light on.

Although this last step, turn your landing light on, is a critical part of standard landing procedure, my instructor pointed out that in the event of an "engine out, off-runway landing at night", you might make an exception. In other words, if you don't like what you see when you turn the landing light on, turn the light off again. If an engine is out and you are crash landing your plane in the dark, you are already in a tough spot, to say the least. By turning the landing light off, you don't know the exact moment of impact because you can't see where you're headed. If you are not tensed up when you make impact, you have a slightly better chance of survival.

Fortunately, I have never had an engine out, off-runway landing at night. I have, however, applied this idea of turning my landing light on—then off again—in my life on the ground. There are distractions and stresses that pop up in every complex, serious situation, but I have a better chance of survival if I can just focus on the task at hand. I do this by using some of the tools in this book: meditating to clear my mind, keeping my mission as my guide, and not getting caught up in what the competition is doing. As a Visionary Leader, you will inevitably face situations that could end in failure. Tune out the distractions, and you might just walk away from a crash landing in the dark.

LEARN TO SURF

"No problem stays solved in a dynamic environment."

—Russell L. Ackoff

THE FIRST DAY OF A NEW JOB is the first day of a job you're going to invent for yourself. You may already have a prescribed job description, and you may have even been hired to achieve specific goals for the organization. However, you are unique, and the experience you have in any job will be uniquely your own.

When I look back on my professional life, I realize that I have had only three major employers in the last thirty-eight years. Still, the number of times I reinvented myself is far greater than the number of positions I held. The world is not static and it doesn't slow down for anyone. Change is a wave, and you can't stop a wave. If you try, you'll drown. What you need to do is learn how to surf.

Whenever you reconfigure a work group or the people in it, you must also reframe and reconstruct how the group functions. An organization is a giant ecosystem that is constantly seeking balance. Leaders need to evolve as the activity inside and outside the organization changes. Having a healthy tolerance for constant change, and even a sense of excitement about the opportunity to reinvent oneself, is a requirement for the modern Visionary Leader.

Reinventing yourself takes ingenuity and creativity, but most importantly, it takes courage. A far-thinking Visionary Leader, one who is looking around the corner or beyond the horizon, often finds him or herself out in front of a significant transition, ahead of the crowd. This space can feel a bit like being stranded in no-man's land, where there is a lot of skepticism and very little company. That's why Visionary Leaders need so much conviction and self-confidence, so that they can move forward anyway and bring entire organizations along with them.

The healthcare industry is currently in the midst of a major reinvention of its own. The Affordable Care Act of 2010 fundamentally changed how healthcare is reimbursed, which means that the shift from volume to value is on its way. We have been working from an unsustainable model for the last fifty years, so current politics aside, healthcare sees a significant change to its payment model. This reinvention will be a rough and rocky one, fraught with setbacks and problems, but the change is inevitable. Those individuals and organizations willing to adapt are ultimately the ones that will be here to see the future.

LET THE FULL EXTENT
OF YOUR IMPACT REMAIN
A MYSTERY

"Never underestimate your ability to make someone's life better—even if you never know it."

—Greg Louganis

IT'S IMPOSSIBLE TO ALWAYS KNOW when you have made an impact on somebody's life. If you get lucky, you'll hear one out of every 100 times that a quick smile, a kind word, or a generous action you've taken has made a difference. Perhaps your words have changed somebody who you will never meet.

Margarita Shields and Russ Miller probably had no idea that they had such a profound impact on my career. I'm sure they would never have imagined that decades later, I'd use their stories while writing a book. You can't measure the true scope of your impact by what you can see. In fact, you can't measure it at all. It's one of those quirks about life that make it so mysterious.

As a Visionary Leader, you are responsible for setting a vision for your employees and indicating the direction for the development of a company culture. Through team discussions and sometimes debate, a singular belief structure and new culture emerges within the organization around the vision. The result is not always exactly the same future that the Visionary Leader had in mind, but it is stronger and more enduring because it's supported by the dedication of dozens, hundreds, or thousands of employees working together toward a common goal. Everyone interprets the vision of your organization via their own thought processes, underscored by their belief structures and experiences, to determine how they are going to own the vision and do everything in their power to achieve it.

I've already talked about the value of developing people and placing a high priority on building self-esteem and higher consciousness in your employees. Having purpose and a goal to work toward can be tremendously valuable to an individual's self-confidence, which sets the cycle of self-esteem in motion. In my career as a leader, I have reached many metrics and achieved many goals. However, the accomplishment I'm proudest of is one I'll never be able to measure: the contributions I've made, however large or small, to increase self-confidence and happiness in the lives of others.

CONCLUSION

IN THIS BOOK, I've introduced concepts on leadership, vision, and relationship to others and yourself. Although these ideas each appear under their own separate headings, they don't function separately in the real world. As you begin to expand your awareness and shift your perspective on what's possible, you'll find that these ideas are inextricably linked with one another, woven into a tapestry that ties them all together. Integrating these concepts takes practice and time, and it is my hope that this book will be only a jumping off point for your journey of self-discovery.

With that said, if I could offer you anything as a takeaway from this book, it would be these core ideas that can indelibly change your life.

1   **Being a Visionary Leader is not a gift.** It is a learned trait that is developed by continually stretching your mind to the possibilities of the future and building the infrastructure to be able to implement your vision when the right time comes.

2 **The first work any Visionary Leader must do is on him or herself.** Start by redesigning your leadership style from the inside out and recognizing that control is an illusion. Find your own sense of self-worth, learn to explore new horizons, dare to charter an unknown course for your organization, and have the audacity to ask others to follow you.

3 **Find the essence of your message and put it in a simple form.** Get right to the heart of what you're trying to achieve and phrase it in a way that every single employee who works for you can understand it. Repeat this message every opportunity you get.

4 **Remember the Success Formula: Create, Commit, Execute.** Create a clear vision of what you want to accomplish, get your organization to understand and commit to the vision, and do whatever it takes in execution to achieve the goal. All principles for organizational success fall under one of these three categories.

If you keep these principles at the heart of how you operate, you'll experience greater success in your business. Even more importantly, you'll be healthier, happier, and satisfied to wake up each day, knowing you are on the journey of a lifetime.

Reading List

Below I have included a small subset of the books which have shaped and informed my thinking over the last four decades. The texts in this list offer a variety of perspectives on mindset, business, and leadership. Starred titles are my particular favorites. I hope you find them as inspiring, innovative, and uplifting as I did.

Biography

Lincoln by David Herbert Donald

E=mc²: A biography of the World's Most Famous Equation by David Bodanis

Einstein: His Life and Universe by Walter Isaacson

Reminiscences by Douglas MacArthur (Autobiography)

Richard M. Nixon: A Life in Full by Conrad Black

The Wizard of Menlo Park: How Thomas Alva Edison Invented the Modern world by Randall E. Stross

Thomas Jefferson: Author of America by Cristopher Hitchens

The Seven Storey Mountain: An Autobiography of Faith by Thomas Merton

Wilson by A. Scott Berg

The Last Lion: Winston Spencer Churchill: Defender of the Realm, 1940-1965 by William Manchester & Paul Reid

Business

Execution: The Discipline of Getting Things Done by Larry Bossidy & Ram Charan*

Re-Creating the Corporation by Russell L. Ackoff

Reinventing the Corporation by John Naisbitt & Patricia Aburdene

The 4 Disciplines of Execution: Achieving Your Wildly Important Goals by Chris McChesney, Sean Cove & Jim Huling

Innovation

Better And Faster: The Proven Path to Unstoppable Ideas by Jeremy Gutsche

Innovation: The Five Disciplines for Creating What Customers Want by Curtis R. Carlson & William W. Wilmot

Innovation & Entrepreneurship by Peter F. Drucker

Juice: The Creative Fuel That Drives World-Class Inventors by Evan I. Schwartz

The Innovator's Dilemma: The Revolutionary Book That Will Change the Way You Do Business by Clayton M. Christensen*

The Innovator's Prescription: A Disruptive Solution for Health Care by Clayton M. Christensen

The Myths of Innovation by Scott Berkun

The Ten Faces of Innovation: IDEO's Strategies for Beating the Devil's Advocate and Driving Creativity Throughout Your Organization by Tom Kelly & Jonathan Littman

Leadership

As The Future Catches You: How Genomics & Other Forces are Changing Your Life, Work, Health & Wealth by Juan Enriquez

Built to Last: Successful Habits of Visionary Companies by Jim Collins and Jerry I. Porras**

Confronting Reality: Doing What Matters to Get Things Right by Larry Bossidy & Ram Charan*

Control Your Destiny or Someone Else Will by Noel M. Tichy & Stratford Sherman*

Corp Business: The 30 Management Principles of the U.S. Marines by David H. Freedman**

Discovering the Future: The Business of Paradigms by Joel Arthur Barker*

Future Perfect: The Case for Progress in a Networked Age by Stanley M. Davis

High Performing Healthcare by Jody Hoffer Gittell

How the Mighty Fall: And Why Some Companies Never Give In by Jim Collins*

Leaders: Strategies for Taking Charge by Warren Bennis & Burt Nanus

Leadership is an Art by Max DePree*

Leadership Without Excuses: How to Create Accountability and High Performance (Instead of Just Talking About It) by Jeff Grimshaw & Gregg Baron

Lightning in a Bottle: Proven Lessons for Leading Change by David Baum**

Lincoln On Leadership: Executive Strategies for Tough Times by Donald T. Phillips*

Management of the Absurd: Paradoxes in Leadership by Richard Farson**

Managing the Future: 10 Driving Forces of Change for the Next Century by Robert B. Tucker**

n=1: How the Uniqueness of Each Individual is Transforming Healthcare by John Koster, M.D., Gary Bisbee & Ram Charan

Outsmart! How to Do What Your Competitors Can't by Jim Champy*

Play to Win: Choosing Growth Over Fear in Work and Life by Larry Wilson and Hersch Wilson

Principle-Centered Leadership by Stephen R. Covey

Reinventing Leadership: Strategies to Empower the Organization by Warren G. Bennis & Robert Townsend*

Servant Leadership: A Journey into the Nature of Legitimate Power & Greatness by Robert K. Greenleaf

Six P's of Physician Leadership: A Primer for Emerging and Developing Leaders by Bruce Flareau, M.D. & J.M. Bohn

Six Thinking Hats by Edward De Bono*

The 21 Irrefutable Laws of Leadership: Follow Them and People Will Follow You by John C. Maxwell

The 22 Immutable Laws of Branding by Al Ries & Laura Ries

The 360° Leader: Developing Your Influence from Anywhere in the Organization by John C Maxwell

The Advantage: Why Organizational Health Trumps Everything Else in Business by Patrick Lencioni

The Effective Executive: The Definitive Guide to Getting the Right Things Done by Peter F. Drucker*

The Five Dysfunctions of a Team: A Leadership Fable by Patrick Lencioni

The Frontiers of Management: Where Tomorrow's Decisions Are Being Shaped Today by Peter F. Drucker

The Leadership Challenge: How to Make Extraordinary Things Happen in Organizations by James M. Kouzes & Barry Z. Posner

The Magic of Thinking Big by David J. Schwartz

The Medici Effect: What Elephants and Epidemics Can Teach Us About Innovation by Frans Johansson**

The New Gold Standard: 5 Leadership Principles for Creating a Legendary Customer Experience Courtesy of the Ritz-Carlton Hotel Company by Joseph A. Michelli

The Paradox Principles: How High-Performance Companies Manage Chaos,

Complexity, and Contradiction to Achieve Superior Results by The Price Waterhouse Cooper Change Integration Team**

The Reputation Economy: How to Optimize Your Digital Footprint in a World Where Your Reputation Is Your Most Valuable Asset by Michael Fertik & David Thompson

The Servant: A Simple Story About the True Essence of Leadership by James C. Hunter

The Speed of Trust: The One Thing That Changes Everything by Stephen M.R. Covey**

The Trust Edge: How Top Leaders Gain Faster Results, Deeper Relationships, and a Stronger Bottom Line by David Horsager

The Trusted Leader: Bringing Out the Best in Your People and Your Company by Robert Galford & Anne Seibold Drapeau

Warfighting by U.S. Marine Corps

What is Lean Six Sigma? by Mike George, Dave Rowlands & Bill Kastle

What the CEO Wants You to Know: How Your Company Really Works by Ram Charan

Winning by Jack Welch

PERSONAL DEVELOPMENT

A Brief History of Time by Stephen Hawking

Absolutely Small: How Quantum Theory Explains Our Everyday World by Michael D. Fayer*

Aikido and the Dynamic Sphere: An Illustrated Introduction by A. Westbrook and O. Ratti

As a Man Thinketh by James Allen*

Contemplative Prayer by Thomas Merton

Creative Visualization: Use the Power of Your Imagination to Create What You Want in Your Life by Shakti Gawain

Crisis & Renewal: Meeting the Challenge of Organizational Change by David K. Hurst

Emotional Intelligence: How They Determine Our Success—Increase Your EQ By Mastering Your Emotions by Dan Miller

*Flow: The Psychology of Optimal Experience by Mihaly Csikszentmihalyi**

Handbook to Higher Consciousness by Ken Keyes

Living in the Light: Follow Your Inner Guidance to Create a New Life and a New World by Shakti Gawain

*Man's Search For Himself by Rollo May**

Meditation for Dummies by Stephen Bodian

NLP: Neuro-Linguistic Programming Techniques For Changing Anything In Your Life Fast by Michael Wright

NLP: Transforming Your Life Today: Life Changing Techniques for Personal and Professional Success by Bastian Ward

Success Through A Positive Mental Attitude by Napoleon Hill and W. Clement Stone

Predictably Irrational: The Hidden Forces That Shape Our Decisions by Dan Ariely

Reframing: Neuro-Linguistic Programming and the Transformation of Meaning by Richard Bandler & John Grinder

Risking: How to Face the Crucial Choices That Will Help You Make the Most of Your Life by David Viscott, M.D.

*Simply Complexity: A Clear Guide to Complexity Theory by Neil Johnson**

Sources of Power: How People Make Decisions by Gary Klein

The Book of Success: Time-Tested Thoughts On How to Enjoy a Rich and Fulfilling Life by Richard Shea

The Executive's Compass: Business and the Good Society by James O'Toole

The Master of Destiny by James Allen

The Theory of Everything: The Origin and Fate of the Universe by Stephen Hawking

The Way of Life According to Lao Tzu as translated by Witter Bynner*

Think and Grow Rich by Napoleon Hill**

Unlimited Power: The New Science of Personal Achievement by Tony Robbins**

www.ingramcontent.com/pod-product-compliance
Lightning Source LLC
Chambersburg PA
CBHW061505180526
45171CB00001B/47